The JOURNAL WRITER'S COMPANION

ABOUT THE AUTHOR

Alyss Thomas is an experienced writer, coach and therapist and has worked as a writing coach for over twenty years. She has helped hundreds of students use journals as a learning tool. This book came to life through her own journalling practice when she discovered she was getting incredible results in life areas she was journalling, compared with the ones where she had not written any journals. She is the author of *The 1000 Most Important Questions You Will Ever Ask Yourself* (Exisle, 2005).

Achieve your goals
Express your creativity
Realize your potential

Alyss Thomas

The JOURNAL WRITER'S COMPANION

EXISLE
PUBLISHING

First published 2019

Exisle Publishing Pty Ltd
PO Box 864, Chatswood, NSW 2057, Australia
226 High Street, Dunedin, 9016, New Zealand
www.exislepublishing.com

A CiP record for this book is available from the National Library of Australia.

ISBN 978 1 925820 04 1

Designed by Gayna Murphy of Mubu Design
Typeset in Cormorant Infant and Minion
Cover image by Annie Spratt/Unsplash
Interior page images from Unsplash
Printed in China

This book uses paper sourced under ISO 14001 guidelines from well-managed
forests and other controlled sources.

10 9 8 7 6 5 4 3 2 1

Disclaimer
While this book is intended as a general information resource and all care has been
taken in compiling the contents, neither the author nor the publisher and their
distributors can be held responsible for any loss, claim or action that may arise from
reliance on the information contained in this book. As each person and situation
is unique, it is the responsibility of the reader to consult a qualified professional
regarding their personal care.

For Joshua and Nathan, who each have
a lifetime to discover the writer within

Gratitude

'As a seasoned journaller of more than 40 years, I can say, hands down, this is the best book on the subject that I have ever read. The whole book flows from one inspiring idea or technique to the next. It is so expansive and beautifully written, that I felt inspired and delighted to incorporate new elements into my own journalling.'

— GRACE CHATTING, PSYCHOTHERAPIST, COACH, FAMILY MEDIATOR AND FOUNDER OF WESTERN WOMEN MEAN BUSINESS.

'I want a lot of copies of this book on my shelf, both to give to people I love and care about but also to support my clients. We are lucky to have this beautiful book to support our creative and therapeutic processes, backed by research and the experience of Alyss who has supported people in their writing and development for many years. She attempts to set us free from the mundane in order to find meaning and beauty in our lived experience through the simple medium of journalling. I highly recommend this book — great for teenagers as well as grannies.'

— DR JOANNA NORTH, CHARTERED PSYCHOLOGIST & BACP SENIOR ACCREDITED PSYCHOTHERAPIST ASSOC. FELLOW & CHARTERED MEMBER OF BRITISH PSYCHOLOGICAL SOCIETY

'Alyss Thomas is passionate about journals and this book fizzes with energy and enthusiasm for the benefits of journalling. Her thoughtful creative book is brimful with useful, practical ideas and inspiration. I love her positive you-can-do-it approach and especially her ideas about journalling as a way of developing mindfulness and becoming more intimate with who you are and what you want. The film maker David Lynch describes creative ideas as being like little and big fish coming to us as our consciousness deepens. This book shows how a journal can help us net more fish.'

— PAUL VALLANCE, REGISTERED PSYCHOTHERAPIST AND ARTIST

'An inspiring, action-oriented yet reflective exploration of the practice, art and craft of journalling. Beginner or old hand, whatever your motivation, goal or purpose in keeping a journal, let this beautiful book be your essential guide and helper.'

— FLORENCE HAMILTON, THERAPIST AND WRITER

'I have long appreciated journalling as a potent tool both for healing and for self-realization. Reading Alyss' insights and advice feels like being guided by a kind and wise friend and her skill as a therapist comes through in the tone, tempo and generosity of care this book offers.'

— RACHEL SINGLETON, BAHONS, PGCE, MLCHOM, ADVEP, DIPTHH, ESSENCE PRACTITIONER AND EDITOR OF *Sentire* MAGAZINE,

'Alyss has kept a journal for most of her life and, in this book, very cleverly and imaginatively shares all the knowledge and experiences she had gained. This is a book full of wonderful and exciting possibilities for everyone.'

— JAN STEWART, ACADEMIC, EDUCATIONALIST AND WRITER

Table of Contents

JOURNAL WRITER'S COMPANION

PART 4: THE BENEFITS OF JOURNALLING

PART 5: BRANCHING OUT WITH JOURNALLING

PART 6: FINAL THOUGHTS

PART 1

Welcome to the world of journalling

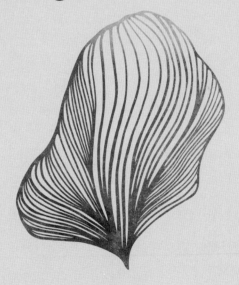

I've kept a journal all my life, as far back as I can remember. I was always excited by the potential of the fresh new journal pages, waiting for my life to open up in front of me.

Preface

As a writer and a lifelong eager student of writing, psychology and the social sciences, I've kept a journal all my life, as far back as I can remember. I was always excited by the potential of the fresh new journal pages, waiting for my life to open up in front of me. In my journal, my writing voice and sense of identity had a space where they could be understood and appreciated. My journal was the one who listened to my active mind, who could reflect and give back to me the truth of who I was. These books were my place to organize my thoughts, and my safe place to explore the edges of all that I was learning and coming to understand.

I kept a few of those journals and when I was reading over them recently I was disappointed by them. It was as if I had no belief in my future self. My early journals had no structure, no organization and no consideration that in the future I would want to read them. The words filled the entire page with no margins or white space, as if I was really short of paper. There were no subject headings, and only occasional dates, and all kinds of material were mixed up together, such as ideas for stories or anecdotes or fragments of dreams. There are two time focuses in a journal — the time when you write and the time when you return to read or review what you have written and take it forward — and I did not take this into account.

WHY I BELIEVE IN MODERN JOURNALLING

I believe everyone has original, unique, quirky, special and unusual ideas, and some special thoughts, experiences or understandings that belong only to them.

If you do not express them, then no one else ever will. There are things you have known or loved or understood in your own special way since you were a young child, and these will have been amplified in certain unique ways by your life experience. I also believe we tend towards social conformity, and we have a kind of herd instinct to fit in rather than stand out, like the wildebeest on the plains. If they all run like crazy at the same time in the same direction across the same crossing point on the river, only a few, the unlucky ones, get eaten by crocodiles or big cats. This conformity prevents a lot of us from freely expressing our weirdest and most private thoughts. If you watch a film of the wildebeest doing this, don't you just want to urge them on? And you get anxious about any straggler who's sniffing out what might be a better and safer crossing point, but she's hesitating because all the others are getting in the water and it's safer to go with the herd. Part of our social brain still behaves like this, and this stifles our creativity. Why?

The direct enemies of your weird, original creative ideas are intolerance, criticism, judgment, fear of ridicule and fear of being unusual and standing out. You are just as likely to reap this from your nearest and dearest, who might gently humiliate or laugh at you or make your ideas sound silly or pointless, as from vicious internet trolls or terrible reviews. We dread exposure that brings the risk of criticism or being humiliated or banished. Yet if you don't have the opportunity to develop your own quirky ideas, so much potential is lost. At the very same time, we are constantly being encouraged to market ourselves, put our ideas out there, promote ourselves, network and be connected and share and monetize our ideas in public — quite a contradiction. This is where the need for a journal arises. Instead of exhorting you to get out there and network, I am suggesting you stay in more and give yourself complete and total permission to discover the 'book' that is your self, the one that you will write as you give yourself the attention, focus, structure, time and space in the special private room of your own that you can create in your journal.

Original creative ideas are not created in public, as this is not a safe space for them and it never was. Look at anyone who has had brilliant ideas and changed the course of history, and you will see they had private incubation space for their ideas. Often they had to ward off disapproval and criticism. They had a room of their own, and in that room they sat and wrote or drew or doodled about thoughts and ideas that anyone else would have judged as preposterous or even heresy. Look at Einstein, who referred to his private space as his 'inner cloister'. If you ever see a photo of his room or his journals, you can see how messy they are because he liked to include lots of different ideas and materials all at once. Virginia Woolf's little book *A Room of One's Own* was written in 1929 but it is just as relevant today. She insists that in order to develop a mind and thoughts of your own, you need privacy, and you may need to assert your right to this. Samuel Morse, who actually invented the telegraph, developed his ideas in his private art studio, and he was mortified about having to reveal them to anyone. He knew his idea could completely change the world of communications, but the idea he created was such a big paradigm shift that he was afraid it would be mocked or rejected.

It's helpful to look at people who became famous for their ideas, as the process worked just the same for them as it does for us. People who succeed in bringing ideas out into the world need courage and self-belief, but this is something that takes time to develop as you work on and strengthen your focus. You have to believe in your early prototypes or vague ideas long before anyone else will, and you must persist in believing in them, just as a mother does with a child. You need a completely private space in which to bring this together, a hidden, internal space protected from opinions, criticisms, judgments or even just casual encouraging comments. If you share your ideas too soon, and expose them before you are ready, they can be lost or lose their potency.

A journal is the private space where you believe in your ideas and your unformed, unknown thoughts. Your journal is where you can be the best version of you that is still in the process of being discovered, where you know you're going to be the best at what you do, and where you are prepared to work away until your projects, your ideas, or your newly minted sense of yourself, are robust enough to be seen in public.

Find your unique passion

three journal prompts

Here are some questions to
take away to explore in your journal.

- What is a secret thing that intrigues you?

- What is something that you loved when you were around seven or eight years old? Go back to that age now and ask your young self to predict their future life, based on the things they loved to do. What does he or she say?

- Reflect on the unusual or distinctive combinations of things you know about. What are the unique combinations of understanding, experience or knowledge that only you know about? In what specific life situations do you have experience and expertise? Write them all down, because you have probably never seen them written before.

A UNIQUE, COMPREHENSIVE HANDBOOK TO SUPPORT YOUR SUCCESS

There are lots of books about journalling, although many of them are mainly about the writer and a specific approach or method of journalling. This book is different in that it is all about you and your journal writing, starting where you are now. The book covers many different journalling approaches, it gets to the point, and there are lots of ideas and techniques you can find easily and apply instantly. I explore a big 360-degree vision of all that modern journalling can be — as a resource that is instantly available to you but is always fresh and innovative. You can use journalling in many different ways, and in the process become your own coach, mentor, supervisor and creative thinker. The book is neither academic and full of references, nor chatty and full of stories. It is a book of ideas, techniques, suggestions, and a comprehensive reference source to many different styles of modern journalling. It's a creative catalyst, and even if you've journalled for years you'll find new ideas here. You don't need to read from beginning to end, but dip in and try something — see page 11 to get you started. You will discover for yourself new ways to open the door into whatever aspects of your being and your life are calling you. It never tells you what to write about, as this already lives within you, but encourages you to find out for yourself what has been waiting for you all along. However, there are plenty of prompts to get you started and to take you far beyond any initial doubt or uncertainty you may feel about the blank white pages that await you.

From the experience of reviewing my past journals, I learned the importance of structuring your writing so that it is a properly organized, positive developmental process that can carry you through all the phases of your life, learning and development. There needs to be an emphasis on courage, structure, positivity and persistence. I have learned a great deal from developing potent new journalling approaches. I have also learned from teaching hundreds of clients, students and coaches to use a journal to support their goals, clarify their thinking and attain results much more quickly. This is the book I always needed as a journal writer but could never find, and the book I have always wanted to give to clients, colleagues and students that will satisfy everyone's needs, whatever they come to journalling for.

The book is based on the principles of positive psychology, and everything in it is focused upon helping you achieve better results and more success, whatever types of journalling you engage in, and whatever topics you are journalling about. It's succinct, with lots of practical tips and journalling prompts and is all about you taking action with journalling in your own life. Thus, the emphasis is not on reading about other people and their stories, but on you as the successful author of your own journals.

I wish for you to discover the joy of journalling and all that it can do for you, in your own time and your own way. However, don't delay. Get started now before you have even read the book. As a reader, you are also invited to join the free, moderated, private Facebook forum 'Journal Writers for Success'.

Get started
with journalling

see flow chart opposite

Once you establish a journal-writing habit, you're likely to find you enjoy it and it brings you more benefits than you expected. Consider this book an advanced training course on journal writing with a purpose. Skip to the parts that interest you and start from there. You don't have to read all of the book. Don't feel limited by the category labels and chapters. Journalling is an apparently simple tool but it is accessible, always with you, inexpensive, infinitely flexible and adaptable. Journalling delivers results and those who journal frequently report enjoyment, satisfaction and the empowering process of learning how to achieve their own goals. Time spent journal writing is time spent investing in yourself, gaining clarity, finding perspective and achieving enviable outcomes.

Interested in bullet journalling? Turn to page 79.

Learn how journalling can benefit your academic or professional life on page 153.

Want to give life writing a go? Turn to page 100.

Interested in shamanic journalling? See page 205.

How do I start?

Learn about the therapeutic benefits of journalling on page 125.

Need some help with the nuts and bolts of getting started? See Chapter 3, 'A quick set-up guide'.

Stuck in a rut with your journalling? See Chapter 14, 'Troubleshooting and problem-solving'.

Want to create a legacy journal? Turn to page 103.

Want to encourage your child to journal? Head to Chapter 12 for ideas.

Refresh your lifelong journalling practice on page 200.

Clean, green, easy and free — journal writing is a free resource that brings life-changing results. In just 15 to 30 minutes a day you can give yourself mindful attention in the special 'room of your own' you create in your journal ... wherever you are.

CHAPTER 1

What can journalling do for you?

Rather than trying to fit yourself into a particular type of journalling, have a think about some things you would really like to achieve, and then look at how journalling might help you. How could you fit in some new journalling approaches with what you do already?

WHATEVER YOU DO, YOU CAN DO IT BETTER WITH JOURNALLING

- Whatever you are aiming for, you can aim higher and achieve more results with journalling.

- If you need more structure — or you need to decompress from a life full of too much structure — journalling can provide both of these (using different approaches, of course).

- Drop old habits and adopt new ones — use a journal space to help you get organized, track your progress and build in friendly accountability.

- Capture the thoughts and ideas that get away — don't lose one more good idea.

- You are capable of fulfilling much more of your potential — but you need tools, education and resources to attain greater success. They're all here in this neat handbook.

JOURNAL WRITING CAN SOLVE EVERYDAY PROBLEMS AND BLOCKS

Journal writing is a new-old method to solve many problems and help you achieve excellence, success and become more self-realized and fulfilled. It is an elegant analogue solution to problems that affect many of us every day. Most of us are:

- busy and preoccupied, and focusing on too many different things at once

- juggling complex demands and trying to be happy and peaceful

- distracted from our underlying sense of purpose, or not sure what this really is

- overwhelmed with information and demands that pull us in different directions every few minutes — this is called being 'busy', and it is how you stay constantly distracted and confused about where to direct your attention

- mentally and emotionally stressed or overwhelmed because of being 'full up' with things to do and think about, while knowing there are some important things we are avoiding or delaying

- online almost constantly

- bogged down or challenged in one or more life areas, and going round in circles or repeating the same mistakes, procrastinating or feeling stuck.

I'm sure you are fully aware you have both the desire and the capacity to achieve or attain great results in life — but greater success eludes you because you don't have a clear method and strategy for making this happen. We need a super effective method for taking control, and although this is not taught in school it is easily within your grasp if you develop a journalling habit.

HOW JOURNAL WRITING CAN HELP YOU CREATE A SENSE OF PURPOSE

Effective and directed journal writing can help you take control of your own thinking, planning and organization processes, and put you in the driving seat. You get to choose what you are going to focus on, develop and achieve.

Journalling is a friendly method to record and keep track of information, ideas, goals, projects and everything that is important to you. Ink it, don't think it — in truth, writing things down is the best way to keep track of everything. But what if you made the writing itself organized, accessible, coherent, fun and enjoyable, rather than limiting your writing to a few to-do lists, a diary or venting your feelings?

You can make substantial changes and improvements in any and all areas of work and life by following the clear guidance and techniques in this book. Energy, focus, attention, clarity, time, health and wellbeing are our most precious assets. Through effective, success-focused journalling you can learn how to make skilful use of these special resources and to value them much more. You'll learn to train your focus on what matters, make the things you want happen, and enable the things you don't want to resolve, diminish in importance or disappear.

Some journal techniques (such as brain dump journalling on page 74) are a way to declutter your mind and get your thoughts straightened out. You can get more of a handle on what thoughts are going around in your mind so you can follow up on the important ones and let go of the ones you do not need. Once you have done this, you can then hone your success in any area of life and work.

WRITING A JOURNAL CAN MAKE YOU HAPPIER, MORE PRODUCTIVE AND MORE FULFILLED

Whatever you want in life, journalling offers you tools to attain it. It is a flexible low-tech and virtually free system to drive success that is available to everyone. If you or someone you care about is not getting the maximum benefits from a journalling practice, try the techniques outlined in this book for just one year, and see the fantastic impact focused journalling will have on your life and your projects.

Almost anyone can gain substantial benefits from journalling. Writing in a journal is the ultimate self-help technique. However, many people who like the idea are unsure how to proceed when facing the blank pages ahead. A journal is often started but never finished, and it does not realize its potential. This book contains, in one place, all that you need to write any form of journal in order to obtain positive results for your life and your projects. It is an indispensable reference book that enables you to create desired outcomes in any area of life using simple and inexpensive tools. All that this process takes is your time, your investment in learning and practising the techniques, and establishing a discipline of writing for 15 to 30 minutes a day. You do not need to buy fancy journals — you can buy any kind of blank notebook, or use an app or a word processing program (see Chapter 6 to read about some different ways to journal).

Can you manage 15 to 30 minutes a day? This might sound like too much, but consider how you might free up this time by reducing browsing on your phone or watching the news. Journalling is the quickest, most efficient way of giving yourself a boost and refocusing your mind on what is really important.

THE RESEARCH IS FRIENDLY

The benefits of journal writing have been researched quite extensively, by psychologists and researchers measuring outcomes for groups of subjects given journalling assignments, compared with control groups who either did not journal, or if they did journal they either wrote about everyday events in a diary style or wrote just about their negative experiences. A lot of different journalling-based research projects point to subjects reporting improved personal outcomes across a range of different research criteria. Because the evidence is there from so many studies, different forms of journal writing deserve to be given much more serious attention as a resource, a treatment option, as a method to improve mood and self-esteem, and as a direct route to achieving one's personal desired outcomes. Various research findings allude to a generally more positive attitude, enhanced mental clarity, increased optimism, increased self-esteem, increased health and wellbeing, a more effective capacity to identify and achieve your deeply desired outcomes, a decluttered and calm mind, an ability to articulate your feelings and thoughts authentically and skilfully … and incredible support in defining, committing to and realizing your goals and dreams.

I could have devoted an entire book to the implications of research for specific journal writing practices, but to keep a strong, practical focus I have kept my theoretical thinking in the background. Please enquire into research on journal writing for yourself, as there is plenty available, and draw your own conclusions about how you can apply this to your own brilliantly useful evidence-based journalling practice! There has been a considerable quantity of research undertaken exploring the effects of different types of journal writing, and the results are not all equal. For example, although journal writing has been demonstrated to improve physical health and reduce symptoms of illness or disease, the symptoms only improve if a specific approach to journalling is taken whereby both cognition and emotions are expressed and there is not too much emphasis on expressing negative feelings.[1]

While any one piece of research can be discounted, the sheer quantity of positive research outcomes concerning journalling deserves our attention. Here are a couple of examples that I have selected randomly. In a study conducted in 2013 titled 'An everyday activity as a treatment for depression: The benefits of expressive writing for people diagnosed with major depressive disorder', researchers found that subjects who wrote about 'their deepest thoughts and feelings', compared with a control group who just wrote factually about daily events, experienced reduction of symptoms of depression that were significant enough for them to recommend journal writing as an adjunct to the established treatments for depression.[2] (This does not mean journalling is only effective for depressed people, any more than exercise is, but this may show that it has potency, as depression is hard to shift.)

Another study that caught my attention was about the effect of emotional disclosure in expressive writing on available working memory. In this study, subjects who wrote about a negative personal experience reported improvement in their available working memory capacity, as well as a decline in intrusive negative thinking, compared with students who just wrote about a positive experience. The study was carefully set up and concluded that 'expressive writing reduces intrusive and avoidant thinking about a stressful experience, thus freeing working memory resources.'[3]

WORKING MEMORY

The reason I find the above study important is that it points to an important benefit of journalling for those individuals among us who carry the tremendous burden of 'low working memory'. Low working memory is something that is often signalled as one component of dyslexia and related issues, and is to do with poor performance in the type of information processing that is necessary for effective planning, and for having a realistic understanding of timing and of time passing. Working memory could be compared with RAM (random access memory) on a computer with a hard drive. The more memory that is taken up with storage, the less is available for the everyday demands of data processing.

So what are the implications for journal writing? Although most of us do not have an official diagnosis of 'low working memory', this is nonetheless a common condition. Many of us experience pressure on our short-term working memory when we are busy, preoccupied, stressed, confused, emotionally upset, unwell, spending a lot of time on social media, feeling overwhelmed, overburdened or over-responsible, or any other factors preventing us from giving our attention to something that we need to follow through on. This is one of the reasons we forget things, and it is the reason we need to-do lists, reminders, shopping lists, ingredients lists and prompts.[4]

GET STARTED WITH THE BRAIN DUMP METHOD

One method of journalling that can help improve low working memory is the brain dump method. If you think you might have low working memory, turn to page 74 and read about how you can get started with this method of journalling, which can help improve short-term working memory.

BENEFITS OF JOURNALLING

Journal writing is the ultimate tool and technique for:

- creating an enhanced sense of purpose
- staying on track with your goals, vision and purpose as these work out each day
- increased wellbeing
- being better organized
- having a system for tracking your goals and targets, and being accountable
- having a designated space where you can realize and express what you really feel and think
- developing ideas
- creating enhanced self-awareness, creativity, productivity and flow
- having a readily available catalyst for success.

Your most precious
assets are your time,
your focus and
your intent.

WHAT YOU NEED TO OBTAIN POSITIVE AND CONSISTENT RESULTS FROM JOURNALLING

Your journals will give back to you what you put into them. The quality, intent, purpose, process and techniques you apply are therefore critical to your success. Surprisingly few people realize the value of this virtually free resource!

You need:

- time, focus and consistent commitment — this can put some people off as they feel they cannot spare 15 minutes a day

- the right materials for you, so that your journal is inviting and easy to use, and your work is easy to refer back to

- ideas and inspiration so that you can't wait to spend time with your journal each day

- education and information about how to use your journals most effectively, in terms of what you personally want to get out of them

- to find a journalling approach, or a customized blend of methods, that fits your context and purpose

- the know-how to set up and maintain your journals in optimum ways so that you experience enduring benefits.

NOTES

....

....

....

....

....

....

....

....

....

....

....

....

PART 2

Getting Started

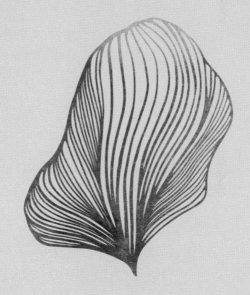

Don't let your inspirations slip away — organize and explore them in a journal. You won't know right away which ideas are special and important, but some of them will be.

CHAPTER 2

Capture your mind on paper

If you have lots of good ideas but can't implement them straight away, or you get ideas in the middle of the night or when you are busy doing something else, you need an ideas journal, a repository of your ideas for future projects. Don't let your inspirations slip away — organize and explore them in a journal. You won't know right away which ideas are special and important, but some of them will be. If you ever see the journals of Earl Tupper, who invented Tupperware, you will see that his journals were full of unusual ideas with detailed sketches and text about scientific enquiries, discoveries and inventions and some of them appear pretty weird — but one of them was for his novel idea of airtight, portable plastic food containers, and also the unique way he invented for them to be sold at 'Tupperware parties' because he could not find another way to get them to his customers.

People tend to believe writing in a journal should be easy and they should already know how to do it, but a little education, guidance and inspiration can make a big difference and open the door to your new life. Many people who gain significant benefits from journal writing follow specific techniques, whether they are aware of this or not. With this book in your hand, you can discover some of the many rewards of modern journalling practice.

A new approach to journalling has grown up in the last few decades. Boring or prescriptive old-world methods have faded away and passionate journallers have re-invented journalling as a grass-roots activity. It's all about hands-on self-empowerment, fusing the best methods available with your own individual interests and needs. Journalling belongs to everyone as a free resource with infinite potential, and many enthusiastic journallers love to share their methods online.

YOUR WRITING VOICE

A person who journals consistently becomes more confident, centred and coherent. Effective journal writing is a portal to finding, defining and refining your voice. Voice in the context of journal writing can be defined as your own unique way of saying things, your expression of your authentic self, the way you realize and express your unique personality and life experience as it intersects with your daily experience of being yourself in the world. When you have the courage to set some of this into written words, your journal writing is an act of determination and courage that changes you because it immediately helps you to engage in further self-realization. People who journal become more self-assured in who they are as individuals. They are more aligned with their own inner-directed sense of self and thus they are aligned with a personal sense of purpose. This may not sound like much, but it is life changing to feel more comfortable and at ease within yourself, and to enjoy expanding your own sense of mission, aliveness, excitement, joy and purpose.

A PLACE TO BE YOU

You are more than the detached narrator of your journals, because your journals are an inside job. You are the author and director of a unique project: writing from your own point of view. When we read a novel we are privileged to be in the mind of the observer, the narrator, or the principal characters, but when you write your journal this privilege is to be in the same room as yourself! You are the owner of the vast territory of your own world, your direct experience of your own reality (rather than what anyone else claims reality to be, based on the observable facts as they see them). In your journal you can claim your point of view and validate your own experience, more clearly and coherently than you may be able to in your relationships or at work or anywhere else. Your journal may be the one place where you can be you, undiluted and uncompromised, without waiting for approval or agreement, and without any hint of comparing yourself with others. It's the place where the prototype models of you and your new ideas and attainments can be sketched out, filled in, modified and developed until they are ready to go public. Do you know what that is like, to put yourself at the centre and constantly investigate further because you know there's so much more potential within you that you can realize if you just put your mind to it? You do, however, need a method to 'put your mind to it' as this doesn't just arise by itself. Journalling is a method for finding out more about who you are, helping you find the very important answers to the basic questions of *who am I and what do I want?*, helping you realize yourself as the author and director of your own sense of purpose, and achieving the individual goals, dreams, fulfilment and satisfaction that belong to you and no other.

When people suggest you 'sort yourself out', 'get over it', 'get a grip on what's important', 'get clear on your priorities', 'get on with it' or 'come back when …', they don't always offer *a method* for accomplishing these massive achievements, which you are meant to summon up — from where? Perhaps you have searched around for systems, theories, organizations, training, therapy or mentoring — to fill in the gaps between what you know you are capable of and what is actually happening in your life. Yes, we all need education and support, but you are already more than capable of bringing yourself into alignment with your own potential. Journalling offers you the least expensive, most direct and uncomplicated method for summoning yourself into being, for becoming more fully, more productively and more happily you, without the need to talk endlessly to friends or your partner. Your relationships cannot carry the weight of your self-exploration, your unravelling, or your need to be entirely self-focused at times — but your journal can. Your journal is the one place where you have total permission for it to be all about you. There has to be one place where it is all about you, because if you don't fully know and understand you and what you really need and want, it is like driving a car where you never get beyond first and second gear. Perhaps you get into third gear, but there is never the sense that you are driving at full speed and testing out the full capacities of your vehicle, tasting the excitement and freedom of the open road.

DEVELOP A CONSISTENT JOURNAL HABIT AND ENJOY THE BENEFITS

You won't experience the benefits until you have established consistency in your journal-writing practice. In doing so, you will gradually discover how a daily writing practice helps develop yourself and your projects and helps bring you results you would not achieve alone. Talk to any long-term journaller and you will find they often secretly long for the moments in their day when they can be with their journal, as journalling is one of the very few good habits that is addictive.

Below are some of the benefits of regular journalling.

- You will experience less self-doubt and be more sure of yourself; if you've tended to rely on others for a sense of direction, approval or advice, you can become more self-reliant and self-directed.

- You develop a clearer relationship with yourself, improve your wellbeing (if you need to) and feel more positive about yourself.

- You can clean up and discharge difficult and confused thoughts and emotions that go round in circles and block your progress.

- Whenever you feel blocked, in any area, your journal can help you to become unstuck and move yourself onwards and upwards.

- Journalling is an excellent way to develop mindfulness, and apply the skills and mindsets that accompany mindfulness, while enjoying the benefits of being more relaxed and centred, and less anxious.

In your journal, as in life, there will always be new things coming up, and there will always be new things to write about. Journal writing is a continual process *of finding the balance and harmony within where you are now.* This constantly changes. With your journal, you can always be on your learning edge and riding the new wave of what you are now becoming and moving towards as you grow and develop. Your journal will always be by your side as a dependable friend and resource to help you be balanced and effective in every situation — but be prepared to change.

PROCESS OVER CONTENT

Your journal is not a product. Most working journals are *process journals*, in that they are about the ongoing process of working with real, present-life material as you live and work through it. A journal is a work-in-progress and its nature is incomplete, imperfect and messy because it is the place where you work things out. Do not feel you have 'spoiled' your journal by using it, or that you 'should' produce something special in it to justify the time you are spending on it. If you want to create a beautiful, ordered or decorated journal, then this is a product, and it is not a process journal, and you will still need a messy process journal to work out much of what will go into it beforehand. You cannot assess the worth of your journal work by how it looks. However, some people obtain great satisfaction and enjoyment from making journalling look and feel good. This is down to personal preference and choice, as well as your abilities, and it's best to follow your own instincts.

HOW WILL YOU JOURNAL?

You can use any medium, or a combination of media, whether you prefer paper journals, a blog or an online writing app. Which do you prefer? Typing is speedier and more efficient and enables you to organize and correct large chunks of text. Online journalling apps can be speedy, fun and efficient. Some people feel writing by hand is more like hard work, or it is inconvenient, or too slow. If you type you can just about keep up with your stream of consciousness, whereas if you write by hand you are forced to slow down. However, the slower, more retro handmade analogue processes of journal writing can be very enjoyable. You are not distracted by all the other things happening on your computer at the same time. The purpose of journalling is not to produce a large quantity of text, but your personal engagement in the process.

Handwritten journals enable you to employ techniques that are more difficult to do onscreen, including doodling, mind-mapping, sketching, presenting your text visually, and adding in numbers, dates, formulas or mathematical workings. Focused and purposeful 'doodling' such as spidergrams, arranging your text visually with frames, boxes and borders, or with more decorative or expressive embellishments helps you to solve problems by using unstructured thinking that uses the creative side of your brain. Writing by hand improves memory recall, encourages critical thinking, helps you to problem solve and to engage in reflective thinking. By grouping your material and organizing it in coherent patterns, you can draw fresh inferences that may not have occurred to you before, because journal writing by hand can nudge you out of exclusive use of linear thinking and help you synergize both hemispheres of your brain. This leads to increased creativity and personal satisfaction in the writing process. For many people, no computerized journal page can replace the pure, open potential of a blank sheet of paper when you are using your journal writing for organization, setting goals, self-expression, exploration and discovery. If you are mainly using it to record a lot of information, however, or you are intending your work to be edited and repurposed, such as a long narrative, typing will be much more efficient.

Even if you are not keen on your handwriting, or you feel bad about it, your handwriting is as unique as your fingerprints, and it is a personal expression of you. If you want to improve your handwriting, however awful you feel it is, you can do this if you are willing to spend time practising. Don't allow the fact that you feel ashamed of your handwriting to put you off because this is something you can work with. Also, if you are not good at spelling or written language, or your work looks untidy, don't let this hold you back either, because in your journal it does not matter at all. You are not following anyone else's rules, and no one is judging. You are writing for your personal growth and fulfilment in your own space and not to please anyone else.

TIPS TO IMPROVE YOUR HANDWRITING

Your handwriting can change if you want it to, and you can find helpful tutorials on YouTube. The most important thing is to have a pleasant flowing feeling while the words are going down your arm, into your hand, through the pen and into the ink that flows onto the paper. The other important thing is that your writing is clear enough that you can read it afterwards, and sometimes these two things can contradict each other, because if you are writing freely and fast it may be hard to read.

There may be some important reasons why writing by hand is stressful, emotional, tiring or difficult for you, or why you write so that no one can read it. You could begin your journalling practice by writing about this and explore on the page what is happening for you as you write, and how it feels. Have a think about how you can work through any blocks and set yourself up for the most success and enjoyment.

When you sit down to write in a journal, ensure you are both sitting up straight and relaxed, and that your writing arm, wrist and hand are supported on the table so there is the least possible tension from your shoulder down through your hand. Experiment with different positions. If you want to improve your handwriting, it is really worthwhile going back to basics, and build the handwriting you want by practising your letters, one letter at a time. Give up on the idea of joined up (cursive) handwriting to begin with, and focus on practising individual letters. Use a guide sheet behind your paper, or use paper with dot grids where you can assign lines of the right width for the size of your writing. Use lines to help you bring in some uniformity to your letter shapes, so all of your letter a's, for example, look the same, are the same size and slanting in the same direction. If you don't like the way they look then experiment with making them rounder, more open or more closed. Work with all the letters that have rounded shapes at the centre of the letter until you feel okay about the shapes you are making. It will take some patience but any practice you can put in will help. Then add the letters that have lines and shapes above and below the line. First try to make them all slant the same way — upright or forward slanting is usually easier to read and write than sloping backwards — and then make the bottoms of the letters such as p's and g's of uniform size, and then the tops. It is okay if, for example, the bottoms of your letters such as q are longer than the tops of letters such as h, as long as they are uniform in size with each other and all facing the same way. When you have practised with individual letters, try joining pairs and threes of letters together with an upward slanting joining stroke that takes you from the bottom part of one letter to the top of the next. You might also consider developing your own flourishes or shapes that you always add to certain letters, such as the way you loop your y's at the end of a word, or the way you dot your i's. The purpose of joined up or cursive writing is that it is quicker and more flowing to write, if you write quickly. However, there is no reason you cannot use non-joined up, printed letters in your journal as you don't have to produce a large quantity of writing in a short time. Art journalling is a fabulous outlet, as the words are only one component and you do not even need to handwrite them — you can use printed words and stick them in.

JOURNALLING APPS

This book is oriented more towards handwriting your journals in a physical book, as there are benefits afforded by the physical writing process. However, every technique in this book can be done onscreen and digitally, and there are journal apps available that make it easy and friendly. Just be careful that whatever app you use makes it easy for you to save, keep and access your previous work. I have not listed all the apps available, or described them in detail, as this is subject to change, while this book will be as useful in twenty years' time as when it was first published. There is a risk that you may be locked out of specific journal apps in twenty years and your data could be lost, plus many of the better journal apps operate by subscription. These all offer versions that are free to download, but to get the most out of them you are locked into subscription software in order to retain your data. They do, however, enable you to include all kinds of media, including photos, audio and video clips, and back up all your data to their servers; such apps include Day One, Moodnotes (which helps you track your feelings over time), Momento (which can import your entries from social media and can turn your Twitter comments into ready-made journal entries; you can also add additional manual entries), or you could try Journey or Daylio.

You could try more open-ended note-taking or word processing approaches that are intended for all types of writing use. You could use Evernote, or just use Google Calendar to create your entries. Using a mainstream word processor like Word feels a bit clunky, even if you might think this would be an obvious choice. The impersonal feel of a word processing program, while essential for producing large amounts of text, may not be friendly enough. Scrivener is a word processing app that is intended to meet the needs of writers, providing you with a 'corkboard' space to gather ideas and themes together. There is, however, a learning curve involved in learning to get the most from it.

Each app has individual pros and cons and, like pre-printed journal books, they provide a pre-formed structure. The advantage is they are quick, stylish and fun to use. However, you have to fit your way of thinking and feeling into their structure, rather than creating a structure that is uniquely customized to you. I feel you can grow and develop your advanced journal practice if you create something uniquely for you, but if you are just starting out, then experiment.

PHYSICAL JOURNALS

Take time in selecting books that are both attractive and fit for the specific purpose of each journal. A spiral-bound student pad would be ideal for a daily pages book. A legacy journal, on the other hand, will need a hardback book. A journal you carry around with you might need to be light, but paperback books don't stay looking good for long if you carry them in your pocket, bag or briefcase unless they are wrapped in a tough outer cover. For planning journals that you will keep, or a bullet journal, a hardback book with page numbering and a contents page section is ideal. Personally I enjoy using Leuchtturm1917 hardback books, which come in a choice of sizes with solid bright covers, ribbon bookmarks, printed contents pages and page numbering and a choice of plain, lined or dotted pages. Other journals include Lemome (great quality), many fine Japanese brands, Moleskine (I wish the paper was a little better, as it always bleeds through, but the feel of these journals is good), Paperblanks (highly decorative, wraparound covers, but the paper is average), Clairefontaine (boring covers but excellent quality fountain-pen friendly paper inside). Traveler's Notebooks are popular and fun, with a wraparound cover you can insert several small volumes inside. You could also create or adapt a loose-leaf system in a ring binder, which gives you much more flexibility.

Consider which page size will make you feel the most relaxed and productive, and whether you prefer lines, grids, dots or blank paper to work on. Personally, I really enjoy faint dots, as they have a finished look, they help to keep your text even and make it easy to draw boxes, headings and create sections on the page. Some paper will accept fountain pen ink, but thin or uncoated paper results in the ink feathering or bleeding through to the next page. Journals with recycled paper can be frustrating if the paper is absorbent and makes your writing look bad, or makes a scratching sound when you write.

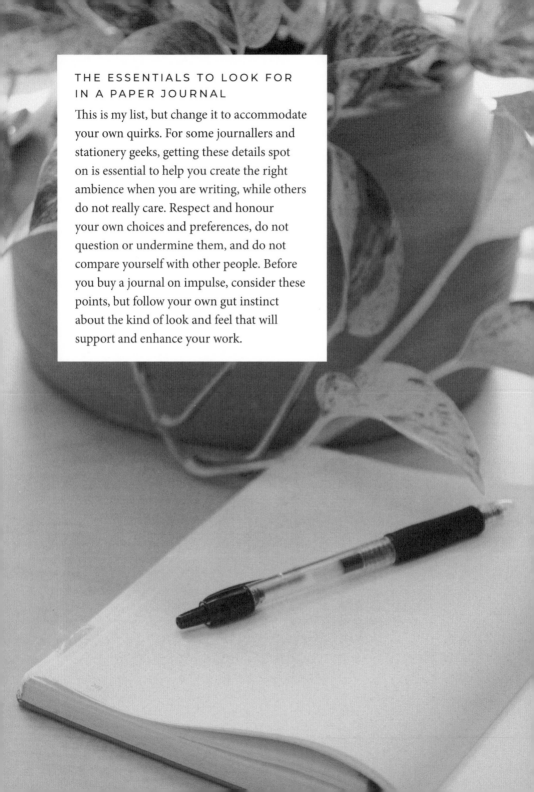

THE ESSENTIALS TO LOOK FOR IN A PAPER JOURNAL

This is my list, but change it to accommodate your own quirks. For some journallers and stationery geeks, getting these details spot on is essential to help you create the right ambience when you are writing, while others do not really care. Respect and honour your own choices and preferences, do not question or undermine them, and do not compare yourself with other people. Before you buy a journal on impulse, consider these points, but follow your own gut instinct about the kind of look and feel that will support and enhance your work.

Purpose, feel and size

The intended purpose for each book for will influence your choice. For example a volume intended as a scribble or brain dump journal can be cheaper paper than a new year journal. However, I have often bought a journal because I liked it and only decided what to use it for after it spent several months decorating a shelf!

The journal must feel good in your hand and make you want to open it and spend time with it. It needs a sufficiently durable cover that inspires you, or that is neutral and that you can customize. The size needs to be appropriate for the size of your handwriting, and the type of journalling project. A book for lists can be slim and tiny, but you may need something with room for growth. You might want a compromise between paper size and portability.

Paper

The paper is really important, as this is where you will be spending your time. It needs to be easy and inviting to write on, and allow you to write and draw on both sides of the paper with your favourite pens without bleeding through too much to the other side. You need your choice of plain, lined, gridded or dotted paper, a printed contents page or index section — or you may be happy to write in your own — and printed page numbers, unless you don't see any problem in writing your own page numbers. A ribbon bookmark or two is very useful, but you could add these yourself. Does the book lie completely flat when you open it so you do not have to hold down one side while you are writing? Will it be difficult to write in the gutter between the two pages because it is curved and not flat?

For an art journal, or any journal with a lot of art elements, you need paper that will cope with what you are painting, drawing, stamping or gluing on it without bleeding through to the other side, smudging or buckling, so use a book with heavy watercolour paper, a scrapbook or craft paper book, or any book from an art supply outlet that states it will cope with the media you want to use. Another option is to glue pages together so they are thicker. Beautiful art journal books are available to purchase, which contain a mix of different types of paper, but they are expensive.

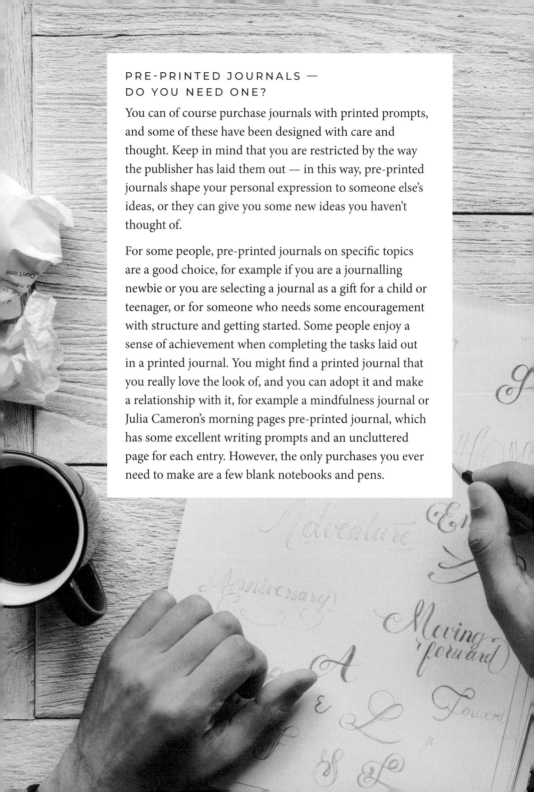

PRE-PRINTED JOURNALS — DO YOU NEED ONE?

You can of course purchase journals with printed prompts, and some of these have been designed with care and thought. Keep in mind that you are restricted by the way the publisher has laid them out — in this way, pre-printed journals shape your personal expression to someone else's ideas, or they can give you some new ideas you haven't thought of.

For some people, pre-printed journals on specific topics are a good choice, for example if you are a journalling newbie or you are selecting a journal as a gift for a child or teenager, or for someone who needs some encouragement with structure and getting started. Some people enjoy a sense of achievement when completing the tasks laid out in a printed journal. You might find a printed journal that you really love the look of, and you can adopt it and make a relationship with it, for example a mindfulness journal or Julia Cameron's morning pages pre-printed journal, which has some excellent writing prompts and an uncluttered page for each entry. However, the only purchases you ever need to make are a few blank notebooks and pens.

PENS

When choosing pens, you may want a range of different colours or inks. You want pens that enable your writing to flow easily and fast, without feeling scratchy. Rollerballs, gel pens, art pens and fountain pens tend to write best. You want the ink to be legible, light-fast and long-lasting. You want to be able to read your writing afterwards, and to balance this with the need for an easy, enjoyable feeling of flow as your hand moves over the pages.

Writing in pencil and some types of pens such as biros won't give the best result. If writing or drawing in pencil is your thing, then consider fixing the work when completed with an art sealant so that it does not smudge onto the opposite page, or fade and become illegible over time.

You have your own creative process and your own ideas, perceptions, thoughts and experiences — they belong only to you. If you don't express them, no one else ever can!

CHAPTER 3

A quick set-up guide

SO HOW DO YOU START?

In order to get started right away before you have even finished reading this book, collect together two or three inexpensive blank books, or open and save two or three computer documents; give them titles and date them. It's good to have a period of experimenting with journal writing, and you will gradually realize what you want your journals to do for you.

Before you begin, you may need to refresh your old ideas about what a journal can be. Many people think of a journal as an old-style 'diary', a place to vent feelings or to make a record of significant events. This is just one of many types of journalling, and it is referred to as 'life writing' in this book. You can, of course, use your journal for life writing, but if you are journalling for success you'll want to use other methods as well.

THE ESSENTIAL UNDERLYING PURPOSE OF ANY JOURNAL

Your journal is a tool to help you become happier and more successful. Whatever your chosen topic and journal methods, the underlying purpose is the same. Your journal is here to help you be more and more fully yourself, to be happy, to be fulfilled, to enjoy yourself and to be successful. Whatever helps you towards these goals is good, and if writing in gold ink makes you feel good then do it, because the entire rationale for your journal is about nudging you towards a more and more positive and enriched mindset. Your relationship with this book is so important, and you need to do whatever it takes to feel good when you write and flip through the pages. If you ever fall out of love with one of your journals, it may be time to close it down and start something new. The energy and personality of the journal has got to feel right.

ORGANIZING, INDEXING AND CLEARLY LABELLING ENTRIES

The key to making all your journal work organized, accessible and useful to you in future is to create good journal housekeeping habits from the beginning. The essential secret to organized journalling is having page numbers and contents pages or an index. Many journal books do not come with these pre-printed so you will need to add your own. Allow plenty of pages for your contents pages. When numbering your pages, you can choose whether to number every page or just the odd pages, and whether to do it all in advance or as you go. If you are using one book for several different projects, then each project will need its own labelling to make it stand out.

Give every single entry you write a title and the date, and then add the title of your entry to the contents pages with the page number/s. When writing your items on your contents pages, be sure to leave several lines of space between each item so if necessary you can come back and write more. Then it is okay if material with the same title appears on different pages all over your journal, as they are all linked together in the contents pages.

You can leave space above your entry to fill in the title later if you are in a hurry because of ideas pouring out or you do not yet know the title, but always include the date at the top of your entry. When you organize and label all your sections, the book becomes very attractive and individual as you start to fill it up, and it will continue to be valuable to you for a long time. For making labels and headings you can use your own handwriting, perhaps adding a frame or a different colour, use stamps or stickers, or purchase an electronic label maker which prints onto coloured tape or ribbon.

When you finish a journal, go through everything to ensure it is labelled and listed in the contents section, then put a label and date on the cover. You can store it in a book box or on a bookshelf, but remember to bring it out and review it from time to time, as it is a precious resource.

USE A VISION BOARD ELEMENT IN A JOURNAL

A vision board is a collection of visual items or text arranged in a strongly visual way and centred on an aspirational theme — something you want to achieve, a lifestyle you want to attain. It is intended to help you experience the feelings of where you are heading for every time you look at it. The visual element invites you to gaze and experience the desired outcome — for example if you are planning vacations every year on an exotic island, or a country home full of space and sunlight, then the colours, items and pictures you assemble create a clear sense of being present in these environments. The vision board does not include the detail of how you will achieve and create these possibilities, but belongs to the envisioning, dreaming and planning stages of journalling. Dedicate some pages to this at the beginning of a journal, so you see them whenever you pick up the journal, to help remind yourself of how you want to feel.

A journal vision board can be non-specific and intended to create a state of mind that you want to experience, to inspire, uplift and encourage you, for example focusing on the qualities of courage, persistence and self-belief, with colours, images from magazines, inspiring quotes, photos or life stories of people you admire.

When you add a vision board element, it will help you bring into focus the underlying intention of modern journalling, which is to nudge you towards a more positive, productive and harmonious mindset every time you see or touch your journal.

A JOURNAL AESTHETIC

Wabi sabi is an aesthetic style well suited to journalling. From Japan, it is nature-based and celebrates the understated, the imperfect and the incomplete. A broken pot of seemingly little value is carefully repaired using precious gold, and kept as a treasure. This look lends itself really well to journals written by hand, that are always in a state of change, are full of changes and corrections, and are never completely finished. The colours in Japanese *wabi sabi* are generally muted in earth-based tones, but there is nothing to stop you adding bright colours as accents. There's an emphasis on observations of nature, on following natural cycles, simplification, and using unpretentious natural elements for decorative details. It is a remedy for perfectionism. Perfectionism is the enemy of the good, the useful and the unformed work in progress. A journal can never be entirely complete. When your journal is almost complete, it is the time to abandon it and start something new. The whole purpose of journal keeping is that you will grow, change and deepen your practice through the process, and the way your journals look will change as well.

For now, choose a look that inspires you and helps you enjoy the time you spend with your journals. There's no need to feel overwhelmed by making the journal attractive or filling it with a lot of decorative details. Some of the beautiful journals you can see online are created by people who work full time to monetise their journals, and while they look super impressive, it is not realistic to try to make your journals look the same.

Successful journalling comes to life in the process of enjoying doing the work. The result is not all visible within the pages of the journal, but within you and what you change in yourself and achieve in life. These are the trophies. Using a lot of decoration might distract you unless your intention is to create something visually alluring, such as a planner that is motivating to use because you love picking it up. Of course, if you have a strong desire to develop your artistic skills further or express yourself creatively, then decorated journalling and art journalling is for you.

A scribble journal

A scribble journal is a scratch pad that goes
everywhere with you and where you can
work things out in rough, jot down ideas
when they occur to you, and work on any of
your projects if you find a few spare minutes.
It is intended to be messy, to be the place
where you start to collect ideas together that
you may develop elsewhere.

To find out more about scribble journalling
and get started, turn to page 75.

Discover the 'book' that is yourself — the one you will write in as you train your focus and become aligned with all that you really love and want to happen.

CHAPTER 4

Journal writing for success

Journalling can help entrepreneurs, leaders, business owners, executives or in fact anyone to increase their levels of achievement and to be both successful and happy. In the approach of *The Journal Writer's Companion* success and happiness are strongly interlinked, and passion and purpose drive them both. Whether you're all about business success or personal transformation, your mindset has the greatest impact on your performance. You can use any of the formats in this book to journal for success, when you hold a deliberate focus on success in your journal writing as an enjoyable and purposeful activity directed towards achieving your desired positive outcomes.

The keys to success include knowing what brings out your confidence, what keeps you motivated and persistent, what helps you train your focus and attention, and how you deal with anxiety and setbacks. People who are successful in any area of life tend to be persistent, and they are willing to learn from mistakes and pick themselves up again as many times as it takes. In fact, successful people tend to make the most mistakes because they make more attempts to make something work, without ever giving up. They never give up on their sense of what is special about them and what they are doing. As they persist in honing their approach and their ideas, their intense focus of attention continues to expand, and this has a positive effect, because they create more and more coherence and momentum for their ideas. Most of all they love what they do and are passionately interested and driven by it, and they do not listen to all those negative voices. Journalling is the ideal vehicle and companion for this work of building up clarity, a sense of direction, and the confidence, power, self-belief and momentum that you need, as well as providing a system for handling all of the information and details you need to keep track of. Remember to keep all of this private, and only share what is necessary.

CLARIFY YOUR DEFINITION, DIRECTION AND PURPOSE

The first phase in achieving outstanding personal and professional growth, success and transformation is increased self-awareness of your underlying thinking and beliefs and what influences your mindset and behaviour. It's more difficult to enjoy success when you're not crystal clear about what really matters to you, you are influenced by other people's opinions or judgments, you get distracted, or you feel reluctant to put effort in. This is like crossing or contradicting yourself with every move you make, and this makes it easy for resistance and procrastination to set in. This is where your journal immediately starts to be useful, as a space to help you gain clarity on what you're all about and define your mojo. Begin each journalling session by firmly establishing yourself in a positive mindset. This is why there has been so much emphasis in journal writing on the idea of the gratitude journal. Gratitude is a free flowing, appreciative and positive attitude, and focusing your attention on the feeling of being grateful is a simple and immediate way to lift yourself up. Simply write about a few things you feel grateful about to uplift your perspective.

WRITE YOUR MANIFESTO

Begin your journal for success by writing yourself a manifesto for each of the important areas of your life and work. For entrepreneurs, business owners and sole traders, crafting a mission statement or an elevator pitch about who you are and what you offer your customers is standard advice. However, I find the manifesto format more uplifting and motivating, and it allows more space for values. A manifesto is a motivational statement that is driven by passion and purpose, that states your intentions, your motives, your vision, beliefs, philosophy, your goals and how you want to put all of this into action. 'I Have a Dream' by Martin Luther King is a manifesto, and the passionately held values within it are still easy to connect with many decades later. So identify the most compelling, the most desirable aspects of what you want to create. A manifesto can help you both talk your talk and walk your walk. Read it over and make revisions from time to time, to inspire you to make improvements, keep up your courage, and keep going.

SOME MANIFESTO PROMPTS

Use some of these prompts to help you kick-start and refine your manifesto/s:

- This is me:

- Every day I:

- I turn W into X through the process of Y.

- This is why I'm here (make this up if you don't know!):

- This is what I want:

- This is what I believe in:

- I am eager to:

- These are my passionately held values and beliefs:

- This is my core philosophy and this is how I want to put it into action:

- This is the world I want to help create:

- These are the problems I can solve:

- This is what (my project) is all about, and this is why it matters:

- I'm changing the way X is done because:

SOME TIPS FOR MAINTAINING FOCUS AND DRIVE

Clear organization, structure and formatting of your journals will really support you. Focus on a few goals at a time, as if you have too much to do you can easily feel overwhelmed and disheartened — and then give up. This is similar to giving yourself such long to-do lists or new year's resolutions that you can never complete them.

You need to bake in a sense of success and empowerment to all of your journalling and implementation processes. List all your long-term, medium-term and short-term goals, but in order to establish a rewarding and productive journalling process, focus in on journalling on just a few areas until you have attained some meaningful results.

In the evenings, build in daily review. Analyze your successes. Reflect upon where you have been successful and made progress, the wins or positive experiences of the day. Focus mainly upon what worked well, and how and why it worked well. Do not spend long cataloguing your fails, because it is more effective to consistently increase your awareness of your strengths and push the boat out further with what is working. Go to sleep with a positive sense of achievement and allow your brain to process the new learning while you sleep.

CREATE AND MAINTAIN POSITIVE HABITS

Much success is built upon a base of positive habits, repetition and nudging yourself towards a better mindset. Start where you are, envisage where you want to be and focus on small, incremental improvements you can make today. Break big goals into small steps — doing one or two small things each day. A belief is a thought about yourself that you keep thinking, and so if you create new thought habits you create new beliefs. You need to hold the positive beliefs consistently to power the life you choose rather than the one that runs by itself, which follows what everyone else is doing, the path of conformity and resistance to your inner self. You can turn new feelings and ideas into new things in your life and work if you focus on them persistently.

A NEW YEAR JOURNAL

There are many reasons why your new year's resolutions may have failed in the past. Perhaps you were not looking at the big picture of what you really want. Maybe the goals were too 'same-old' and didn't stretch you enough. Maybe they were driven by logic or necessity, and you weren't paying attention to your intuition about something new. Maybe you were not aligning with the highest part of yourself. Another possible reason is that you didn't have a solid plan of action in place to back up your goals.

New year — and you decide when your personal new year is — is a perfect time to begin a new journal. Hopefully you will have some holiday time in which you can set up a new journal that will last you for the year ahead. This year, instead of making resolutions you don't stick with, journal your resolutions and plans and see the difference this will make!

According to Philip Clarke at the University of Derby, a key problem in sticking with new year's resolutions is that while it is relatively easy to decide what you would like to achieve in the coming year, many people give themselves very little help, structure or ongoing support for actually achieving these goals — they don't really think it through or build in easy methods to achieve them.[1] Setting goals is important, but it is just the beginning of the change process, and it can't work all by itself. The process of journalling and writing down your goals sets you up for a more successful outcome, if you then use a structured journalling approach, with built-in reviews and accountability, and with a positive focus on something that motivates you and that you know you can realistically attain.

A survey of 2000 British people found that many people are not confident they can set and stick to new year's resolutions, but they agreed that setting small, achievable goals could make a difference.[2] The University of Derby study team suggested that those who develop effective action plans for achieving their goals feel greater confidence and satisfaction, and are much more likely to succeed. At the same time, any action plan you create must be created in such a way that fulfilling it is satisfying.

NEW YEAR'S RESOLUTION ACTION PLAN

The most important thing to open your new year planning is your to-be list, not your to-do list. This is all about how you want to feel this year, who and what you are going to honour, nurture, pay close attention to and enjoy in order to be joyful, happy and aligned to the best of who you are. Before you write any resolutions, spend time in your journal reflecting on the bigger picture. Happy is the new successful. Wellbeing is key to success. What will help you increase your happiness this year? What can you do to ensure as much happiness as possible? What nurtures your greatest sense of wellbeing, and confidence in yourself that all is well? What are the goals you can get behind without a sense of resistance and struggle? What can you plan for this year that will make you feel good? How can you use your time to feel whole, happy, well and aligned with your values and your inner sense of purpose, rather than attempt to be ruthlessly efficient? How is it that different people achieve vastly different results within the same time? Those who are more successful are engaged with passion, and enjoy the journey as much as the destination. Therefore they have less resistance and the planned activities do not clash with their values or sense of purpose.

Taking the time to dream big and plan your goals in your mind is an essential stage in starting anything. The way in which you express it to yourself and write it down, however, is critical to your eventual success. Your goals need to be exciting, fun and as motivating as possible. You need to write your goals from the vantage point of having already achieved the outcome. For example, if you intend to make $20,000 additional revenue this year, visualize yourself spending this money. So write your goal of bringing in the extra money in terms of how this is going to make you feel — for example, 'I'm really excited that we're going to be able take a trip to Bali in September.' For a new year's resolution, you need a goal that is attainable within one year or less, and so this could be a subset of a larger goal, for example that you will save a certain sum towards the house that you are not going to be able to afford this year but within the next three years. You will always need a mix of longer-term and short-term goals, with a blend of projects at different levels of difficulty. The goals you choose need to be specific, so that it's really clear what you need to do in order to achieve them. For example, if you write that you intend to lose weight, this is not specific or motivating enough. Write that you plan to lose a specific amount of weight by a specific month, how you will do it

with simple guidelines to remind yourself to follow, and what the outcome of losing this weight will be — you will feel more confident and attractive when you go on your holiday, for example, and you will buy gorgeous new swimwear or sunglasses to celebrate.

It is important when setting such goals that they are realistic and attainable. It is self-defeating to set goals you will find difficult to attain when you are busy, tired or preoccupied. In setting unrealistic goals, it is as if people vaguely hope that a miracle will happen, but they do not offer themselves the support, infrastructure and motivation to enable success. It is also important you do not set yourself too many complex and challenging goals at the beginning of each year, because you do not want to have the experience of failing at them. It is better for you psychologically to achieve a few manageable goals, and then review and set new targets as you are able.

Make sure your goals can be achieved realistically in the timeframe you set for yourself. It's discouraging if you keep failing to meet targets, so set yourself targets that feel easy so that when other stuff happens in life, you don't drop the ball. When you have achieved this, set a new target that's a little more difficult but that does not engage your resistance. Set a specific date by which you want to achieve each goal, and write this date into your planner. For long-term goals you can have targets that you review after a few months, and by having some short-term goals you always have something that is up and coming to focus on and motivate you to succeed. There is nothing like success in meeting goals — it is the best feeling, and it is highly motivating in helping you move on to the next goals that then move into your reach. This is a key component of the action plan. You want a balance of challenge to keep you motivated but not so much that you lose focus and feel stressed. A suggested guideline is to increase your goals by 5 per cent each time you reach a target, so you work in 5 per cent increments.

If one of your new year intentions is to be more organized, keep track of your goals and your to-do list and track your progress as a way of moving forwards, then bullet journalling may work well for you. You might want to incorporate some bullet journal strategies into your new year planning, such as tracking your progress in changing a habit. For more information on bullet journalling see pages 79–84.

Many of us think up some fantastic goals and ideas but we forget them. So 'ink it once you have thought it'. By recording your goal or idea, exploring it, and then going back to review it, you make a more definite commitment to it. It's good to spend time with new ideas, turn them over in your mind, scribble and sketch about them and make them yours. This is exactly the way in which amazing new ideas are invented or created. Thomas Edison's journals are an example — they are full of all kinds of ideas, and one of them became the light bulb.

SMART GOALS

When you are creating — or reviewing — your effective new year's action plan, use the 'SMART' acronym. SMART is short for goals that are Specific, Meaningful, Agreed upon (i.e. you are fully committed), Realistic and that exist within a Timeframe. SMART goals are easy to understand, and you know when they have been accomplished.[3]

S = Specific

M = Meaningful

A = Agreed

R = Realistic

T = Time Frame

Some new year journalling prompts

- A new year journal could also become your yearbook, a motivational planner or organizer that includes all the planning elements you need tied in with diary elements and monthly spreads.

- You can use a bullet journal format or purchase a planner if you can find one where the structure, layout and design appeals to you. Spend time on choosing the best format, organizing and decorating it. This can become an annual ritual, with each year's book building and improving on the last.

- Journalling is for life and not just for new year, and you are going to set yourself up for success. Name your journal for the year, and perhaps call it your yearbook, your goals book, or any name you find appealing and motivational. Here are some suggestions for format and contents for your yearbook.

- Create a motivational vision board for the year ahead — a planning spread with visual elements. This could include space for financial goals, ambitions, professional goals, continued education, personal intentions, physical health, your social, community and friendships, intimate relationships, family and roots, creativity, fun, work–life balance, trips and events.

- Write in personal reminders of why your goals are important to you.

- Create an individualized mind map or spidergram of all you want to attend to and accomplish over the coming year. Write the year date in a circle in the middle of the page and write all your areas of focus in spokes around this hub. Review this each month, as a way to renew and refresh your focus. What you give your time and attention to is what will grow.

- Focus on how you feel when writing your goals. Write goals that make you feel happy and aligned with the authentic you. Then when you review them over the year this will help you maintain a positive outlook.

- At the end or beginning of each year, take time to review how the previous year went. List your wins, what you did and achieved, what changed, what you learned, perhaps activities you engaged in. List what you want to let go and leave behind with the old year. List what you want to take forwards.

- Write a personalized 'mission statement' for the year ahead, stating the definition, direction and purpose of your major goals.

PART 3

Different types
of journalling

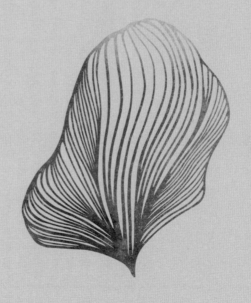

You might think your own life is ordinary and nothing special, but so did all the famous journal writers who used their journal writing to invent, create and transform the world.

CHAPTER 5

The history and philosophy of journalling

In this chapter, we begin by taking a brief look at a few well-known journal writers from the past, in order to understand modern journalling approaches in a wider context. Then we will go on to explore some modern approaches.

Many gifted people have been lifelong journallers, and their journals have survived: such as Marie Curie, whose journals are still radioactive because she carried radioactive polonium in her pocket; Einstein, whose journals cover a vast variety of subjects and are messy and untidy; Darwin, who documented his findings and observations about the natural world, and stored them in a series of numbered notebooks; Leonardo da Vinci, who saw no problem in blending annotated drawings of his discoveries and personal diarizing on the same pages. He wrote from right to left, and his diaries can only be read in a mirror. Beatrix Potter wrote detailed observational diaries of the nature and wildlife that she loved from the age of fifteen, with sketches and paintings, but the words were written in a code that was only unlocked after her death. She wrote incredibly detailed observations of the natural world, and through close and careful recording and curiosity, she discovered new information about biology and natural history that naturalists still rely on. This was the background that provided the context for her memorable animal characters in her famous children's books. Mark Twain filled every inch of his pages with an ongoing and highly detailed commentary on every aspect of his life and times. The collected diaries of Samuel Pepys begin in January 1660, and reveal far more about the texture of daily life, attitudes, relationships and the preoccupations of the day than any history book.

You might think your own life is ordinary and uninteresting, but if you journal about it the process will help you to look at your world more carefully, to be more curious, to record extraordinary details that only you can perceive and describe, and convey your values and philosophy of life. In the recovered *Diary of a Farmer's Wife 1796–1797, Anne Hughes, her boke in wiche I write what I doe, when I hav the tyme, and beginnen with this daye, Feb ye 6 1796*, we see a glimpse into the life and times of a young countrywoman who found moments to write — before her first child was born — while her husband was out, as a kind of forbidden pleasure. This book was — supposedly — handed down and discovered in the twentieth century, and published first in *Farmer's Weekly* and then by Penguin Books in 1981. There is some doubt about whether the book is genuine or a sophisticated fictionalized fake, but nonetheless it is a fascinating read. 'I have not writ in my little book for manie days, not feeling verrie well. John's mother did bid me to cum to my bed chamber to rest, so I do get my book out of the linen chest where it be hid, and do rite.' After one year she says there is so much to do that she will not have time to write anymore but she will keep her book safe, as she would like to pass it on to her children. She wonders who will read her book in the future, and she also hopes that they will be as happy as she feels in her marriage. For her, the writing was a secret pleasure and not something she could take for granted. She reveals so much about social attitudes, village life, her relationship with her husband, and how she cheerfully manages his grumpy moods. She shows a sense of wanting her work to be a legacy, that she was living and recording a special moment in time and yet was worried that those around her would think she, as a busy farmer's wife, was wasting her time on something she was not entitled to participate in. Her life and times are forgotten, along with all the hard work she did, but her words remain, and with them her resilient and positive attitude and her genuine and exemplary kindness to all who were less fortunate than herself.

Perhaps the most famous journal is that of Anne Frank. The writing of a thirteen-year-old girl, it was written when she was hiding with her family during the German occupation of Amsterdam during World War II. She begins, famously, '… it seems to me that later on neither I nor anyone else will be interested in the musings of a thirteen-year old school girl. Oh well, it doesn't matter. I feel like writing.' The writing stops abruptly in August 1944, when her family were discovered and sent to Auschwitz. However, her words remain with us as her father, the only survivor of the family, published her 'diary' in 1947. She did not write it in a traditional 'dear diary' tone, but wrote to a fictional friend, already aware of her potential audience. Her father had perhaps never realized the depth of her understanding and her capacity for self-expression. Anne's work is full of an awe-inspiring resilience and a sense of purpose that sets the experience of our own lives into context. It is possible that she was inspired to write because of hearing a radio broadcast encouraging people in the occupied territories to write diaries and documents that could be read in the future.

There is also Victor Frankl's work, rewritten after he left Auschwitz as his first draft was destroyed by the Nazis. Writing when he could, on scraps of paper while he was incarcerated, helped him find a purpose for surviving and he wanted to share what he was discovering about the strength of the human spirit. His work, published under the title *Man's Search for Meaning*, is an exploration of what is important in life, what creates true strength and resilience, and what real happiness and success are built upon.

Writings like these help us see our own lives in a different light. They illustrate the journalling 'voices' of ordinary folk who were determined to make something from the living texture of their day-to-day experience, and who often had to write in secret. In doing so they uplifted themselves and found a great sense of purpose in the writing, not even knowing if their writings would ever be read — many years later their distinct personal voice and experience continue to uplift generations of readers across the world.

We see these writers clearing their minds and orienting themselves within their lives and times, using the experience and ordinary everyday concepts available to them, and their voices emerge with a distinct clarity. It is as if they pour everything in, and then what is important rises to the top like a cork bobbing on the surface. We tend to think our own ordinary lives are dull and have no significance, and that only famous people are interesting. But these journals and books were written by ordinary folk who had the drive to write and who were honest — the early publishers of Anne Frank's diary felt it was necessary to censor her reflections about her emerging sexuality, and it has been banned in several places. The specific, real details of anyone's life are fascinating if told in an authentic voice. If you write down what you notice, what you notice will be unique and different. When you look back over your entries after some time has elapsed, you will see material you can develop and work on that you didn't realize was there. 'Writing in the round' is a way to describe writing that is grounded and centred in your own experience, from the unique point of view that only you possess, as if you are sitting in the middle of a circle and writing about the entire circumference around you.

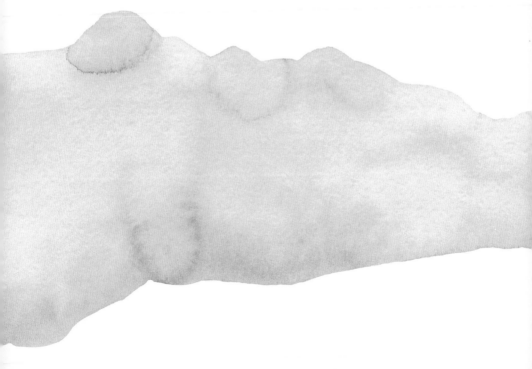

Modern journalling encompasses many different types of journalling, and is of course not limited to writing about your life. There are many different ways in which keeping a journal can enrich your life and your own sense of your place in the world. You can make your own unique combination of style and methods, and what's important is your personal living, dynamic relationship with your journalling life where you are truthful, authentic, present, engaged and generous with your time.

A journal is where your new life
begins, as you capture your new sense
of self that unfurls like a new leaf.

CHAPTER 6

Modern journal writing for coherence and creativity

This section is intended to help you think about journalling in some new ways, and there are some ideas to get you started.

One of the most productive aspects of journalling is that it can help you become more successful in any area of life through a process of *entraining your coherence*. The idea of coherence implies that all the different aspects of us are integrated so that they work alongside each other and all head in the same direction. This is all about focus. In a journal you can develop, step by step, a constructive attitude, and build your strength, momentum and clarity. One of the most basic and enduring challenges that can severely limit success in any area of life is that we hold ideas, beliefs or thoughts that are contradictory. You can see the evidence of this where you hold an intention but you do not follow it through, where you want something but you do not take the appropriate actions to bring it about, or where you engage in behaviour that is erratic and inconsistent because different aspects of you are not working together in a concerted, coherent sense of direction.

To understand inconsistent, contradictory motivations and behaviours, we have to accept the existence of parts of ourselves that are less mature or less developed, more fearful or resistant and less forward thinking, which are motivated by feelings that we are not always consciously aware of. We say or intend one thing, but what we actually do is not aligned with our intention. Thus, the single most important function of journalling is to bring yourself into a state of harmonious, positive coherence and focus. Journalling is a powerful tool for (a) training your focus on the things that really matter to you, and (b) consistently improving your state of mind. Working with your resistance wherever it shows up, such as in procrastination or underperforming, takes both patience and self-awareness on your part — but you do not ever have to take your resistance and contradictory thoughts or behaviours at face value. Push through them rather than allow them the space to take over.

Journal writing can help you make order and harmony across all the different areas of your life experience. If you feel out of balance, or you don't understand something about yourself, you can work it out simply by writing about it with the underlying intention that you seek to move through this and find increased wellbeing. If you take the time to do this, the different aspects of yourself will come together on the page, all working consciously and collaboratively towards the same goal.

USE JOURNALLING TO SET THE TONE YOU WANT

Whichever method of journalling you gravitate towards, and whatever your topic, productive work emerges when you are in the creative zone of flow. This requires space and focus, but even just 15 minutes each morning can set you up for the day. When you first wake up is good because your mind has not yet started to fill up with thoughts. Mozart is frequently quoted as saying 'when I am completely myself, entirely alone and of good cheer … my ideas flow best and most abundantly'. To be in this zone, you have to create the condition of 'good cheer', be present and attentive; do not force anything but instead be receptive.

Some of the ways you can use journalling

- To define your intentions: to express yourself, organize yourself, clarify your thoughts and feelings, develop greater coherence.

- To create a vision for your purpose and of your success.

- To clarify the 'why' that underlies your sense of purpose.

- To plan your desired outcomes.

- To track, observe, monitor, maintain or improve wellbeing or a specific goal or needs.

- To collect, collate and curate ideas, information, notes and records.

- To give you greater leverage in a task, assignment, job or project.

- For self-reflection, self-awareness, self-mentoring and mindfulness.

- To create a document, record or creative work.

- To ease you into a state of engagement and flow.

- To improve your mindset and reach for more positive, courageous thoughts and outcomes.

- To identify your self-limiting beliefs.

- To take control of your thoughts and feelings.

- To help you commit to taking appropriate and timely action.

- To build positive momentum.

- To support you to follow through on your decisions.

- To take action on the feeling that there is something more that you want to be doing in life.

- To bring you zest and fulfilment.

TWO METHODS TO GET YOU STARTED

Start journalling straight away. Here are two simple methods you can try out: the brain dump method and scribble journalling.

BRAIN DUMP

Journal writing can help any of us improve our short-term working memory capacity and this means it will help us to become more crisp and focused when we need to be. One journalling method to achieve this is the 'brain dump' method, where you write down everything that is on your mind, and all that you are feeling. By putting it down on paper, you release it from your working memory so your mind no longer feels it has to hold on to it all. *Now the journal, diary, phone or computer is holding this vital information for you, and you don't have to.* This explains why writing a daily, weekly or monthly to-do list is so useful — because you have written it down, you no longer have the stress and anxiety of holding it active in your already over-burdened working memory. Instead, you can relax because you have captured it, and you have more capacity to go ahead and actually start completing the items on your list.

The only way to find out if this process will work for you is to try it out for yourself. For one month, spend time each day deliberately writing down what is on your mind. Then do a quick scan through your body and also write down any emotions, feelings or sensations that come into your awareness. Do not get into discussing or analyzing any of this data as you write it down; you are just going to dump it for now.

At the end of the process, write a fresh to-do list for today, and then get on with your day. For this to work effectively, you need to do it every day (don't worry if you miss a day here and there), with consistency and regularity. You will need 15 to 30 minutes for the process. You should not spend more than this, because you are not here to write an essay and get caught up in all this material. If you do find that material is emerging that really wants your attention, then identify and section off that material. Designate it for a different type of journalling process that you will undertake at a different time and in a different way. During the brain dump, a few really good ideas will, apparently randomly, spring into your mind as if from nowhere. Write down these ideas to capture them, and go back to them when you have time. After the month is up, go back and review what you have written and compare your state of mind, your working memory capacity, your mental clarity and your effectiveness in following through on important tasks now, compared to when you started. Do you notice any differences? If so, you may then be able to hone and customize the process so that you can use it to deliver to yourself the most important benefits over the next month.

You can take an empirical observation approach to your personal journal writing practice. Over the course of a year, try some of the journalling processes in the book, and observe the effect they have on you and your success with your projects. Develop your unique combination of journalling methods based upon what works for you, and get clear about what journalling techniques work for you. Observe carefully how you think, feel and perform after your journalling sessions.

SCRIBBLE JOURNALLING

You can practise journalling and writing ideas to see how they will look if you take them further, practise layouts and compositions, write first drafts or practise handwriting styles. Label and date each entry, and label and date each scribble journal when it is full, and archive it until you are sure you have migrated important ideas on to new journals.

When you are busy, a scribble journal may be the only journal you manage day to day during the week, but keeping one is the essential underpinning of an effective journal practice. A scribble journal provides you with one place to capture all kinds of thoughts, ideas, exercises, notes and things you want to remember. When you feel like writing but you don't know what you are going to write, you want to vent your feelings, take some space to recover from an unpleasant experience, or you want to write something you know you won't want to keep long — this is where to start. A spiral-bound student notebook where you can easily remove pages is a good option or perhaps a plain notebook that goes with you everywhere.

Capture your wild and random thoughts: some scribble journal prompts

Take a scribble journal and write down everything that is on your mind. This is a process of emptying out all the contents of your mind. Write down everything that comes to mind in response to each of the prompts below. However, write it down fast and then move on to the next item — don't spend long on any item. For this exercise you only have to list your thoughts but not look into them in any detail.

- The things you are thinking about.

- How you are feeling.

- How you feel about your health and wellbeing.

- How you feel towards your family members.

- How you feel about your work.

- Anything you are worried about.

- Anything you feel dread about.

- The things you are hoping will happen.

- The things you are looking forward to.

- The things you have been doing today and what you are doing tomorrow.

- The things you ought to do but may not get round to yet.

- The things you definitely have to do.

- The things you need to remember that you might forget.

- Some enjoyable things you would really like to do if you had the time.

- Some nice or positive things you would like to remember to do or think about when you get round to it or when you have the time.

Now go over all of this in different colours and cross out anything that is not that important and you can forget about. Then highlight anything that has come to light that you want to retain. Circle anything that is important that you attend to, whether immediately or longer term. You might want to migrate these items to a different journal, when you have decided what type of journal/s you are going to keep.

DIFFERENT TYPES OF JOURNALLING: FOUR MODERN METHODS

Here are four different types of journalling to explore. If one of them appeals to you, there are extensive resources you can find online, but there is enough information here to get you started, and so that you can compare four completely different approaches. You can see that when different people talk or write about journalling, they are not always discussing the same things.

BULLET JOURNALLING

A bullet journal is the ultimate task manager and productivity assistant. If you struggle to keep your task management, lists, schedules, reminders, random thoughts and jottings and vital information under control, the bullet journal can change your life! There are so many people who have adopted variations of this system because they are tired of having bits of information scattered across different apps and notebooks. For many people it has replaced a large number of different productivity systems, especially for those of us who multitask across many different aspects of work and life.

Bullet journalling is popular across the globe and has many different variations and applications. Because there is so much information online, starting a bullet journal from scratch can appear overwhelming and complicated. However, it was never intended to be like this. The system is completely logical, and the best advice is to keep it very simple while you get used to it, then you can customize it when you know exactly what you want from it.

The bullet journal was intended to be minimalist and to require the least possible amount of input from you in order to support you to stay productive and on top of your game. It is neat and organized (that doesn't mean you have to keep it tidy) and if you also want a self-expression journal, this would either be separate to your bullet journal or an indexed part nesting within it and contained within designated pages. Bullet journalling was developed by Ryder Carroll, who struggled with focusing and holding on to lots of information at once due to low working memory and a poor attention span. He wanted something to enable him to keep track of diverse and complex information in an accessible, visual format that was quick and easy to review and update each day.

Bullet journalling is ideal if you want to simplify a busy life or job, or streamline lots of diverse information into something that is visual, clear, trackable, organized and efficient. You can track something such as weight loss alongside business topics, and your bullet journal (or BuJo, as they are often called) treats it all the same. A bullet journal is like a personal assistant for your mind and projects, and it provides a practical method of curating, managing, pigeonholing and staying on top of your ideas and tasks, both long-term and immediate. It is an elegant and efficient way to stay on track with everything so you don't drop the ball on one project when another takes up most of your attention. Above all, it helps you see how and where you are spending your time and energy, and it helps you focus on what most matters to you.

Ryder Carroll has made his ideas freely available to everyone, and anyone can develop their own variations and additions. Variations of the bullet journal enable people across the world to stay on track with their goals, tasks and targets. It is perfect for managing any information you want to monitor, observe, track, record or evaluate. This organized system provides you with a visual reference of all your ideas, plans, notes, tasks, reminders, appointments and more. In addition to this, working within the BuJo format constantly encourages you to streamline your working process, to focus on what matters, to be consistent in achieving your goals, and to leave behind anything that turns out to be unimportant. A bullet journal is a structured hybrid between an organizer or planner, a diary and a journal, and everyone's bullet journal looks different.

You can find information at bulletjournal.com, and there is also an app and a book, but here is the basic information for trying out your own bullet journal.

How to use a bullet journal

First you need a suitable notebook. While you really can use any notebook, the 'official' standard bullet journal format is a medium sized, plain black hardcover notebook of 248 pages, with a four-page printed index at the front, four pages for your 'future log', printed page numbers, a printed key of symbols, and tips and instructions. If your chosen book does not have an index or page numbers, you need to write them in, as this is integral to the system. Dotted or squared paper is more useful than lined paper as it gives you more accuracy and flexibility.

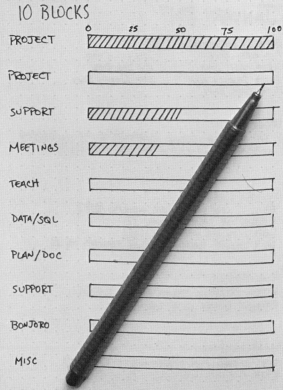

10 BLOCKS

	0	25	50	75	100

PROJECT
PROJECT
SUPPORT
MEETINGS
TEACH
DATA/SQL
PLAN/DOC
SUPPORT
BONJORO
MISC

MONDAY
10:00 NEWBILL UPDATE
11:00 TEAM MEETING
1:00 QUEUE SPRINT
2:00 NEWBILL MEETING

TUESDAY
10:30 ENGINEERING
2:00 WORKSHOP
3:30 BARRETT

WOO!

WEDNESDAY
1:00 QUEUE SPRINT
2:00 FB LIVE
4:00 NASHVILLE MLS!

ONE BIG THING

SHIP IT.

THURSDAY
10:45 SUCCESS MEETING
1:00 WORKSHOP
2:30 PICKUP CANAAN

FRIDAY
10:00 BOOK CLUB
11:00 STEVEN
1:00 QUEUE SPRINT
5:00 REVIEW WEEK

The index is the heart of the bullet journal system, and this alone makes the system of 'rapid logging' possible, as you add to the index every topic area that you add to your journal. 'Rapid logging' refers to a key aspect of bullet journalling, meaning that you write down all your tasks, ideas, schedules and information fast, in list format. Once they are written down, you can go back and work on them on another page when you are ready to. The system of 'threading' means you can also place an arrow next to the page number, on the bottom-right of each page, with the page number/s of where the current topic continues. You don't leave any blank space in your bullet journal when you change focus or topic; you simply write on the next blank page and note everything in the index so you can always find entries.

First, you need to establish a simple system of visual 'bullets', which are basic symbols — you draw in one of these bullets next to each of your list items. In addition to the bullets, you need a selection of further symbols to accompany the bullets, which denote different types of status for all of your tasks — thus all actionable items are given a code in addition to the basic bullet. First you itemize them as a task (the basic bullet) then as you work through them you add variations of further symbols to signify whether they are 'scheduled' with specific dates, whether they are an event, whether they have become irrelevant, whether they have been 'migrated' (which means they have not been completed but have been moved forwards to the next time period), or if they are completed. Of course, many tasks might require numerous subtasks, so you will need a special page for these. You need a variety of symbols to denote events, notes, priorities, appointments and so forth, and a way to indicate when they have been completed. You can create your own symbols/signifiers as I have done in the example, or adopt the ones Ryder Carroll suggests. Put your legend for your symbols at the beginning of the book in case you forget or want to add new variations. Date your book with the year and month that you start, for when you archive it.

The 'future log'

The bullet journal begins with your 'future log'. This is bullet journal language for forward planning written in the form of a list. Simply list all your ideas, goals, things you want to achieve or monitor over the period of time this journal will cover, whether this is a few months or a year or more. List one future intention per line, in brief factual language, such as 'lose 3 kilos by June'. Whatever the topic, and whether it is personal or business, you list it in the same brief, factual way, in any order. This is an excellent way to capture all of your ideas about things you want to do, experience or complete at any time in the future. Once they are written in your future log list, those you do not complete in the timeframe of this journal will be 'migrated' to your next bullet journal, so they will never be completely lost or forgotten. When you work on something, then you add a new symbol to the log, or strike through the item when it is completed.

The 'monthly log'

This is all about your calendar, diary, dates, goals, reminders, processes and intentions for the month ahead. Begin by writing the name of the next calendar or lunar month on the left of a double-page spread. (This is an opportunity to be decorative; for example some bullet journallers allow a full page for an embellished and inspiring introduction to the month, perhaps with a seasonal theme or uplifting quotes.) Down the left-hand side of the left-hand page, write the days and dates of the month in two simple adjacent columns, in the format F 1 for Friday the 1st. (You will need to copy the dates from a calendar.) Add the page number and name of the month to your index or contents pages at the front of the book. Write things you need to remember next to the dates, such as deadlines or appointments. Again, everything is written briefly, whether it is a meeting, a haircut or the day you plan to propose to the one you love! If this format does not allow you enough space — if you have a lot of events and appointments — you could take one page each for half the month. If you have a lot of appointments (for example, client appointments), a monthly log might not replace your appointments diary, but you can then keep a simple appointments diary and cross-reference any important information.

The right-hand page of this spread, or the next separate page, is a monthly 'task page' — write down everything you can think of that you want to attend to this month. These two sections provide a quick visual reference for the month ahead that you can refer to frequently. Don't write in the next month yet, because at this stage you do not know how many pages this month's logs will take.

Your 'daily logs' and 'collections'

Instead of having the same space available each month, as in a regular planner, you can take as much or as little space as you need for any entry because the next page is always blank. In the next pages, start your daily notes, called your 'daily logs', and your various project notes and trackers, called your 'collections'.

This is where you can create quick and easy tracking charts for anything you want to monitor or improve, such as self-care. As an example, you can create a food diary. Record everything you eat over a period of time, and log how it makes you feel, whether you feel energized or not, and how it affects your weight. You could keep a list of different foods and record how they affect you, or a list of foods you want to include in your diet, along with simple recipes. As soon as you begin to collect this information in a simple and easy-to-read chart, with symbols, you will see much more clearly what you are eating and drinking, and the effects it has on you. You can also create charts for distances you walk or run, gym-based targets, or targets for weight loss or gain. By focusing on important details of self-care in this way you'll become more aware of your habits. With this increased awareness and focus, it is much easier to overcome procrastination and nudge yourself daily towards increasing health and wellbeing.

You can also create 'collections' pages for specific projects. Your collections can be fun or useful or both, such as books you want to read, bucket lists, a timeline for the next phase of a project, your gratitude diary, birthdays, or people you want to connect with.

Although the bullet journal is the ultimate resource for the overwhelmed, you might feel overwhelmed by the process itself to begin with, and the sheer choice of things you can do with it, so give yourself permission to experiment in your first bullet journal and adapt the various processes to fit your needs, rather than trying to fit in to someone else's version of what a bullet journal is. Your bullet journal is ideal for keeping track of everything in one place, both work and personal, as well as detailed workings out on specific projects. The bullet journal idea continues to evolve and expand, but in essence it's all about feeling satisfied and fulfilled by being organized, being in control, and having easy access to all your essential information.

DAILY PAGES JOURNALLING

Many people practise the 'morning pages' journal, an idea made popular and successful by Julia Cameron in her worldwide books and teachings on the 'artist's way'.[1] In her books and lectures, she describes in detail this form of journalling that she calls morning pages, as she recommends you do it first thing in the morning while your mind is still clear, and that you write three pages per day. Morning pages is form of journalling that has specific functions and is a form of writing known as free association writing. Although it is unstructured, it does have a purpose. Julia Cameron has been practising it for decades, and she reports many benefits, and she claims that it has been the basis of her worldwide popularity as a writer and workshop leader. This is worth considering in your own situation. Over many years of practice, Julia has been able to distil the essence of what is important to her about this form of daily journal writing and she conveys it in her popular books, which have brought many people to modern journal writing. You can find out more about her approach to morning pages or try out the slightly different and adapted method I use that I refer to as daily pages. This is similar to a scribble journal (see page 75), in that it is just a record of whatever is going through your mind that day. However, it is different to a scribble journal because the focus is more on your 'stream of consciousness' and it is a method for downloading whatever is going on in your mind rather than for capturing everything you want to attend to or do. It is almost the complete opposite of bullet journaling, and the mood is spacious and reflective rather than brief, efficient and organized.

'I wake up in the morning and my mind starts making sentences, and I have to get rid of them fast ...'

ERNEST HEMINGWAY

To follow the daily pages process, write freely about whatever comes to mind for a short time period each day. You do not need to choose a topic in advance, and you do not need to spend longer than 15 minutes, but it should be a daily or frequent practice. The important focus of the exercise is just to keep writing. Write about how you feel, or thoughts and ideas that come to mind. You can simply describe your immediate sense impressions, such as what you can see, feel and hear in the room around you. You can write about your dreams, pink fluffy unicorns, a conversation with a friend, or your ideas for a novel even if you have no intention of actually writing it.

The daily pages routine is all about the writing process, and not about the content of your writing. In fact, do not pay too much attention to the content, but instead focus upon maintaining the flow of your writing. If you find yourself completely stalled or stuck, then write about the experience of being unable to write, or use one of the prompts on pages 90–91. Although there is complete freedom about what you write, there is nonetheless a strict form related to persistence and regularity. It is also best if you are strict with the timekeeping and do not go on for longer than 20 to 30 minutes, as this is a way of learning to manage the process of writing down your unconscious flow.

Think about the message this conveys to your subconscious, that you are writing something every day, and that you are treating your journalling process seriously. It doesn't matter whether you feel like writing or not, or even whether you have anything to say. It doesn't matter if what you write is complete rubbish, in your view. The purpose of daily pages is not to write anything brilliant or even acceptable. It is about being entrained to the journalling process. If you keep to this simple discipline, you will notice how changes occur over time. First of all, the thoughts and ideas circulating in your mind now have somewhere to go, and you will make a new space for fresh thoughts and ideas. This is an important clearing out and decluttering process for your mind. We have so many thoughts, conversations, sense impressions, responses to news and media going on all at once, and you might never realize how important it is to clear all of this out so you have a fresh, clean space to start again.

At times you may find yourself writing about strong feelings or views that you might not want to share with anyone. It's important that no one else reads this journal; it is your own private domain. You can always destroy the pages. In writing daily pages it is important not to be critical about what comes out, and not to censor yourself.

Daily pages can help you settle in to your writing voice. Often we don't know what our writing voice is until we have the experience of writing in different ways and finding what feels most true and authentic. Daily pages are like warm-up exercises for the rest of your journal writing. You are not expecting them to look or sound good or to be important productions in their own right, but the process of the exercise is strengthening.

Daily pages can be helpful at certain times in your life, when you need an outlet for self-expression or you need to clear your mind, or when you need to keep your writing in flow because you are working up to a big project. It is really like attending a gym for your mind, so that other journalling processes or work that you undertake will come more easily because you are keeping the flow going.

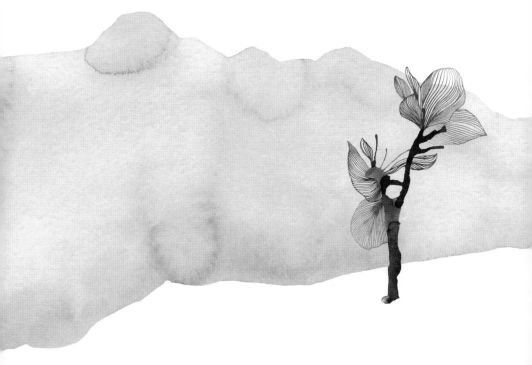

Daily pages journal writing is ideal in the following situations:

- When you need to write for work, business or university, or because you are a writer or need to stay in flow with your writing, keep the ideas flowing or build your confidence and momentum.

- You have the feeling you want to keep a journal, but you are unsure about how and where to begin.

- You feel confused, anxious or depressed and you have no idea about how to start unpacking what is on your mind; daily pages is a way of unburdening your mind — by putting it down on paper, you can release mental and emotional material that has been weighing down on you because it has had nowhere to go.

- You are bursting with ideas but you can't capture them and they are elusive or keep going round in your mind, without anything happening, and you are not able to put them into action.

Instructions for daily pages

Assign a large notebook just for your daily pages practice. It can be anything you like but you need to feel you can write freely and there is plenty of space.

Create a fixed time each day for this exercise. It is important to get into a routine; for example, write with your morning tea or coffee. Once you establish the habit, you will quickly realize the benefits such as feeling more energized, or an increased sense of wellbeing and clarity. Try this for at least six weeks.

It is important to have respect for the routine, and to treat it as a special, mindful activity. Set up your writing space and materials so it feels nice and cared for. You are showing up for a special assignment with yourself each day. This care and respect will signal to your 'unconscious' mind that you are now ready to listen, and you will record it for 15 to 30 minutes a day, without judgment, criticism or interference from your rational mind.

Begin each entry with the date. You could also include local conditions such as the weather, your situation, and what you are currently dealing with in your life. This will make it interesting to read much later on as it will provide a context for what flows onto the pages. At the end of each entry, leave a few lines of space before the next.

Review your daily pages

Put your writing away at the end of each session and do not review it immediately. After a few weeks or months, read through all your entries and highlight anything you would like to repurpose or explore further. Again, do not engage in criticism or judgment of the writing you produced while you were clearing your mind and dumping out the contents. You can copy any items you would like to keep or explore further into a different notebook. Note anything that intrigues you or that you didn't consciously realize was happening. What is the difference between your earlier entries and what you are writing now?

An additional technique for daily pages

Try writing some of your journal entries with your non-dominant hand. This technique is used to encourage self-expression of the non-linear aspects of your consciousness. Persist with it, as it can feel awkward and uncomfortable to begin with. One way to do this is to ask a question written by your dominant hand, and then answer the question with the other hand. The writing will probably be messy and hard to read but it's a way to open up flow and obtain a different perspective.

How are you feeling right now?

Describe your immediate physical environment and what you can see, feel, taste, touch and hear. Use descriptive words rather than making judgments.

Prompts for daily pages

Describe someone you feel attracted to, someone you love and admire, or someone you dislike or feel angry with.

What are you feeling confused about or clear about? What do you feel convinced about?

Report on your feelings and thoughts following a situation/event/discussion that just took place.

What is most important in your world right now?

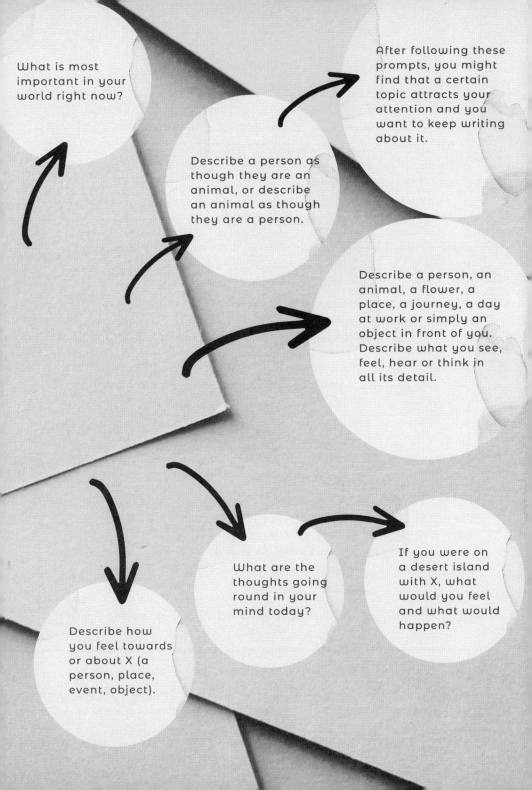

Describe a person as though they are an animal, or describe an animal as though they are a person.

After following these prompts, you might find that a certain topic attracts your attention and you want to keep writing about it.

Describe a person, an animal, a flower, a place, a journey, a day at work or simply an object in front of you. Describe what you see, feel, hear or think in all its detail.

Describe how you feel towards or about X (a person, place, event, object).

What are the thoughts going round in your mind today?

If you were on a desert island with X, what would you feel and what would happen?

ART JOURNALLING

Art journalling is the ultimate form of personal self-expression. Art journalling is a fusion between expressive personal art and journalling, and is a form of personal creativity like no other. You can blend journal and artistic elements within an overall theme, where decoration, self-expression and meaning interweave and support each other. An art journal is both a product and a process. It's hugely enjoyable and satisfying to create and provides a fantastic opportunity for your creativity, and at the end you also have a book that is lovely to hold and look at.

The more traditional form of 'artist's journal' is the artist's notebook or sketchbook, which is often a collection of studies, or a series of observations in both sketches, paintings and words such as 'the wildlife in my garden'. The art journal is a thing in itself that blends ideas, words and visual elements in a thematic way using mixed media. You can find plenty of inspiration online, with many gorgeous examples of art journal pages created by talented artists.

The process of art journalling is tactile and immersive because you work with three-dimensional materials and processes: paper, collaged papers, gesso, glue, paint and ink, and you are stamping, painting, tearing, gluing, glazing, printing and colouring just as much as you are writing. The richness of all the media creates a high level of sensual engagement and enjoyment that is very different to writing on its own. If you are a visual or artistic thinker, or you are experiencing limits with writing but you really want to journal, then art journalling can be deeply absorbing. Explore YouTube and Pinterest, and copy other people's ideas in order to get started. In the end you will find your own style and approach based upon what pleases and intrigues you. As in all journalling and self-expressive work, you find the way forward by following what excites, intrigues and delights you, not by following anyone else's rules or process.

If you have yearned to be artistic or to paint or draw, but felt you weren't able to, art journalling will welcome you as it is a level playing field and you do not need an art education. You don't have to be able to draw or paint, as you can use collaged or stamped images and just have fun discovering all that you can do, because anyone can join in. The qualities you need, and that you can develop further in art journalling, are curiosity, playfulness and willingness to discover where the experience will take you. To start exploring art journalling, you need a blank book with robust art-worthy paper, such as heavy watercolour paper or craft paper, or a purpose-designed art journal. You can also make your own by stitching together signatures — sections of folded pages — within a simple handmade cover of card covered with papers or fabric, and held together with masking tape; or you can even repurpose an old unwanted hardcover book by removing some pages, and then painting over the remaining pages with gesso to make room for your own material. Always test your materials on your paper first, just in case something does not work well.

Mixed media techniques give you the freedom to explore materials you personally enjoy; while you are enjoying yourself, you will over time find and create your own style. You can combine acrylic or watercolour paints, crayons, pencils, markers, inks, stencils, masking, stamping, collage, decoupage, washi tape, photos, illustrations, newspapers and magazines, and bought and found embellishments such as tickets, trinkets, dried leaves and flower petals, ribbons, decorated tags, or any small items you have kept. You will need supplies including gesso to prime and seal your pages, and an acrylic medium, or Mod Podge, which serves as a glue and sealant to cohere all of your items on the page with a uniform finish.

Get started with art journalling

Choose a general theme you would like to explore and assemble some visual elements and some words relating to the theme. It is best to begin with a simple colour scheme of no more than three main colours, plus black and white and perhaps metallic highlights. Take time to really enjoy the process, although many art journallers like to work quickly and assemble their pages without allowing themselves time for logical thought or analysis. Go with what you like and enjoy, and don't engage in critical thought. A theme can come to you from anywhere, such as a dictionary, a quote or something someone says, or the fruit on your kitchen table.

Create a background to work on. First, prime your pages with gesso to create a neutral, even surface that can then receive all your different media — that is, unless you want to work with watercolour on watercolour paper and the fluidity of wet paper. Then build a background, for example by starting with some layers of found papers or a patterned paper that you love. Use some transparent papers such as tissue, vellum or tracing paper to create layers and depth. You can build a background based on colour, for example using layers of acrylic paint, stencilling and stamping. If you make a watercolour background each layer needs to be sealed after each colour is laid down and dried, so that the layers remain distinct. You can make interesting backgrounds with watercolour paint by covering a wet page of watercolour paper with blobs of watercolour, and then dropping some drops of isopropyl alcohol (rubbing alcohol) into the wet paint. The paint will separate and make an attractive marbled effect. It is effective if you have two tones of the same colour and then one or two contrasting colours, but stick to colours either in the warm or the cool spectrum, as there is a fine line between flow and mess! Where the paint pools or runs too much you can gently remove some of it with kitchen paper. You can modify the effect by blowing the paint though a straw or lifting the page to make the paint run. Once it has dried and you have sealed it, you can add to it, such as by flicking metallic paint from a loaded brush over the page, drawing lines with a marker, or writing.

Your background should have elements of mystery within it, for example text that is only half-seen or intriguing layers, or words that invite curiosity. It is the context for the subject matter or theme you are exploring. Once you have created your background, create a border to contain your page and bring it together. Your border could be created from small, regular sized pieces of magazine photos, a stamped or stencilled pattern, or a simple hand-drawn pen and ink or pencil frame, or a frame made from geometric patterns. It can be loose or tight depending on your theme. Once you have a background to your pages, add different elements in layers. For the base of your pages, use patterned papers, washi tapes, collaged magazine pictures, pages from old books, photos, newspaper, letters or any found papers. Blend them together with acrylic medium, perhaps tinted with a little acrylic paint in a colour such as Titanium Buff, a light neutral colour, to give you a coherent base on which to start adding your layers.

Now you have your background and your border, assemble your visual items on the page, before sticking them down, to see what they will look like and play around until you have a pleasing and harmonious montage that feels right to you. You need to have a main subject or focal point in the foreground, and a play or inter-relationship between background and foreground.

When you are happy with the overall design, you can begin to attach your items with layers of medium. It's best to brush out any air bubbles, but wrinkles are okay as they can add to the texture. If you want a heavy textured effect, you can build this up with some acrylic texture paste pushed through a stencil. Then you can add your words, which can be printed and cut out, stickers, collaged words from newsprint or hand written. Remember, you want to leave yourself an inviting and attractive space to write in. Some people create an art journal and then go back and write in it after they have finished designing it. You can glue on words and paint around the edges to blend them in, or glue a decorated envelope or folder onto a page, within which you can store a little notebook, tags or papers for further 'secret' writing.

Finally, seal your page again and add final decorative items such as lines, sparkles, highlights or final words, or emphasize some elements by drawing around them with a fine tip brush pen.

Ideas and techniques for beautiful art journal pages

Collect materials you can use such as pictures from books and magazines, or raid your own old photos that are sitting around doing nothing or drawers of trinkets or sewing materials.

If you want easy themes to get you started, create pages based upon natural themes, such as clouds and rain, sea and sky, summertime or winter trees. You can combine these themes with images of people and activities, such as a small figure walking with an umbrella, falling leaves, raindrops or spring skies and cherry blossom. Create a journal based upon how you experience the passing seasons, using colours and themes that stand out for you. You can always start with one item you really like, such as a piece of washi tape or patterned paper, and use these colours and tones as the base for your theme.

Create a page based upon one or two words or feelings that are evocative and positive for you, that you would like to immerse yourself in, such as nostalgia, happiness, flow, harmony, balance, abundance, wellbeing, creativity, open door, journey, family. Use art journal pages to create mood and vision boards of experiences and feelings you want to feel connected to. Immerse yourself intensively in colours, images and feelings that help you re-align to new and exciting ideas, or territories you are claiming for yourself such as health or wealth, where you want to live, the work you want to do or peace, joy and enlightenment.

Create a page based on one or two colours, and allow yourself to enter into the heights and depths of the colour, or the relationship between the two colours, and focus on how you feel when you are in this colour space. This can have incredible results, even if you just use black and white (hint: only use the tiniest dot of diluted black acrylic paint, as black soon takes over). Write on the page about your feelings about being in this colour space, how it affects you and what it brings to mind.

Use torn pieces and strips of newspaper as a unifying background, and create a series of pages with simple themes on a newspaper base. See how much atmosphere and mood you can create using simplified elements and materials. Or use your own words, printed out and sealed with an acrylic medium or Mod Podge.

Create something entirely new and unexpected by bringing together an assortment of themes, ideas, colours, textures, words and images you like but that do not have an obvious connection, such as astronomy and diet, a haiku and management. Use found text from contrasting publications. Try pale pink pastels balanced with structure and organization, or a grid balanced with floral scrolls, playing with ideas of contrast and difference which still reveal an underlying coherence.

Create your own monoprints using a gel printing plate — a gelli plate — to print your own layered backgrounds to cut up and add to your journal pages. This is easy and fun. You can purchase or even make your own gelli plate, and use a rubber brayer to apply acrylic paint or inks to the surface. You can use stencils and masks to add texture, either bought stencils or leaves, feathers or household items such as plastic wrap or bottle tops. When a print has dried, you can add further partial or translucent prints on top. If you use stamping inkpad inks such as Distress Inks on the plate, you can also stamp directly on to the plate. Lay the paper over the gelli plate, smooth it down across the plate, and lift off — you have a beautiful print with lovely details from the stamps. Watch this process on YouTube to see just how addictive it can be. You can use watercolour paper or even much thinner paper depending on how much ink or paint the paper can handle.

You can paint over pictures cut from old magazines or books, if you first seal them with acrylic medium, to transform them into paintings and blend them into your page. There is not an issue with copyright if you are altering these images for your own personal use.

You can use royalty-free images you print from the internet. If you use an inkjet printer, this ink is not waterproof so you need to seal it before you can put anything on top of it. Laser prints are less volatile if they get wet, but you still need to seal them.

Collect together items that relate to or express aspects of the themes you want to journal about. It works well if you have at least three different pieces of texture or illustration to blend that look as though they belong together — for example, they might all have red in them — and then a focal point to bring balance or contrast.

Don't forget to allow plenty of space for your writing by creating an inset space where your writing belongs. Many art journal artists do not allow much space for the words, which are treated as one of several decorative elements. As a journaller using art journal techniques, you will probably have more to write and give the writing more priority on the page. The art components make your writing more expressive and more complete and also express aspects that are harder to capture in words. You can use words in a looser or more poetic way, or use found words, or journal on a theme suggested by found words such as in a newspaper or magazine article.

If, on the other hand, you are not so comfortable with formal writing, in art journalling you do not have to write proper sentences, or even make sense. An art journal is more like poetry than prose or continuous text. You can express yourself freely or write lists or families of words. Do not judge or criticize your work, as it is a step along the way, not intended as fine art. It is a process of engaging play and expression through which you will discover something.

Have a look at some examples of art journalling online to see the range of possibilities. A book to get you started is *Art Journal Kickstarter* by Kristy Conlin.[2] The book includes examples from 150 different art journallers, and you can clearly see what materials and techniques they use, how they found and developed their ideas, and the processes they enjoy. It will give you a sense of the range of possibilities, and at the same time you will see how achievable and accessible art journalling is even if you feel you have little artistic ability.

Tap into your creativity
beyond words. An art journal
is not about perfection but
free self-expression, and
having a creative centre to
curate your ideas.

LIFE WRITING

Life writing — writing about your life — is what many people think of when they think of journalling. It can also be described as keeping a diary and is a perennial form of journalling. You don't need any instructions or guidance to simply write whatever you feel about what has been happening in your life, but you may want to emphasize certain aspects in order to leverage the most benefit from the writing.

If you enjoy writing a few paragraphs or pages a day and you don't always know what you'll be writing about before you begin — or you get the urge to journal but you are not attracted to a specific topic or approach — life writing may be for you.

WAYS IN WHICH YOU CAN USE LIFE WRITING

Daily life can pass by in a blur and you will soon forget all that is vivid and fresh today. Capturing and recording some of your immediate and recent life experience brings perspective. Rather than just being immersed in your life experience, you can reflect and write about it as you go, which is different to talking about it. Journalling about a trip or a relationship as you go through the experience enriches the experience, and gives you material you may be able to use later. Journalling what is going on for you on days when there are significant world events can make fascinating reading a few years on. The life writings of the journallers mentioned earlier are as fascinating for the characters' awareness of what was going on in the wider world as they are for the intimate details. Writing your life is a creative act in which you meet yourself on the page and choose how you respond to your circumstances.

There are different motivations for life writing. You can write for clarity, for insight and reflection about your day-to-day experience, and to explore your thoughts and feelings. You can create a record or diary of what you are living through. You can write the story of your life over a specific period of time, such as the first year in your life as a parent, or a recollection of a period of your childhood. What are the stories that only you can tell and the unique, extraordinary memories you hold? Writing about yourself is fun, satisfying and enabling if you do it in productive ways. It is not so much about recalling events, but about writing from your experience and making space for the expression of your unique sensibility and awareness.

WRITING THROUGH, OR ABOUT, DIFFICULT EXPERIENCES

Writing can be a way of finding yourself and your authentic voice when life is tough. Words can conjure hope, resilience and courage. Some journallers and writers find themselves in a struggle to form and reform themselves. Sometimes there is an experience of blankness, or absence, where you know your harmonious, authentic self-expression should be. You have to wait for it, poised on the edge of the abyss, feeling as though you're doing nothing, while all the work happens internally; you are reorganising and re-integrating but there is nothing to show for it in the outer world and you struggle to find any words that feel flowing and alive.

Writing so that you take control of your material can be a catalyst for change.

WRITING TO VENT YOUR FEELINGS

You might want to simply express your feelings, such as your frustration about something that isn't going well, feelings of loss and bereavement, or writing in the voice of your wounded inner child. This can provide release and help you come to terms with situations and how you feel. This is not likely to be writing you will want to keep — but what comes after you have released the pressure may be. Do not stop at releasing your feelings but go on to consider what you have learned from these experiences, how you can move forwards from here, and how you have overcome obstacles and setbacks.

Hold in mind that the purpose of this type of writing is to increase self-awareness and resilience, foster a growth mindset and encourage your positive forward momentum.

A few life writing prompts

- Set yourself specific themes and describe episodes and memories from childhood. Examples might be family holidays, the places you loved, your relationships with animals or pets, the things you knew to be true as a child that no one told you, or what made you feel most alive and excited. Bring back as much detail as possible. The more you focus on describing what you can remember, the more you will be able to recall. Stay within the themes, as this will give your writing a coherent shape and will stop any tendency to ramble.

- Write your life as you want it to be; enjoy the satisfaction of creating exactly what you want.

- Celebrate all that is positive in your life.

- Describe your current life as though to an extra-terrestrial — step outside and look in with the eyes of someone who does not have your assumptions about what is ordinary, normal and everyday.

- When you have been on a trip, write as soon as possible after you come home about how you see your life just as you are stepping back into it.

- Write a brief story of your life as though you are the hero or heroine in your own novel or movie script. Focus on how you want this to turn out, and on how the beginning already contains the seeds of the fulfilment and satisfaction that blossom in the later stages.

- Explore ongoing themes such as relationships, parenting or career focus across different generations of your family, including your ancestors as far back as you can go, the newest members of your family, and your own life experience in these areas.

DO YOU WANT TO CREATE A MEMOIR?

Are you ready to share your story with the world, or with a selected audience? Do you have a story to tell? Life can indeed be stranger and more incredible than fiction, and your story could inspire others. There are many amazing memoirs and autobiographies written in a variety of styles, and you might want to read some examples for inspiration. An autobiography is a story of your whole life, whereas a memoir is focused on one or more aspects of your life, defined by a theme or a timeframe.

If you think your story would be something others might enjoy, then you need to shape your material for your intended audience. Divide your material into chapters and sections defined by chronological sequence, themes, events or relationships. Label each chapter and subsection clearly, and help your readers find their way around your material by being a good host who shows them around and thinks about their needs. Don't just write about yourself from your own inside perspective, but consider the effect of what you are writing on others. If you want to share your work, think about whether you can make your writing accessible and enjoyable for your readers. What kind of reading experience do you want them to have?

LEGACY JOURNALS

A legacy journal is a record, a product you create to keep or to pass on. If you want to create a legacy journal as an artwork, as a record, or perhaps as something to pass on to younger members of your family, you will need plan it out in advance. The work needs to be created in rough form before you transfer it to your legacy journal. It could, of course, include edited excerpts from your process journals. You can journal the entire planning process in your process journal, as a project.

There are many reasons why you might want to create a legacy journal, and it can be a very satisfying hobby. You could create a family history, or a statement you would like to be handed on through the family. You might consider getting the book printed through a company such as lulu.com who help you create e-books and can also print copies on demand that you can then distribute. If you follow this route, the work must be correctly formatted. You could also consider producing a printed photo book. There are companies that offer online templates, where you upload your photos and captions into a pre-designed format, and then order copies.

You can also create a legacy journal for someone else, by working alongside them if they cannot not do this on their own. You can interview an older person and ask them to tell you their memories, and then record them. With a child or a person with a disability, the process of creating a book all about them can be empowering and help them develop an increased sense of self, and pride in what they have accomplished. When you are working with someone else in this way, you will need to find a balance between providing a structure that you either design yourself or that you create together, and allowing the person to take ownership of the project. You do not want to stifle a child's creativity by being controlling; nor do you want to leave them alone with a blank book. In working with someone else, the key principles are offering regular sessions, kindness, acceptance, witnessing, accompanying them on the journey, and being willing to offer resources, ideas and support. The sessions can be a fun and enjoyable way of affirming your relationship and having some precious one-on-one time together.

You could create a hybrid between a process and a legacy journal, such as a travel journal where you document your daily experiences and include souvenirs and illustrations — a curated journal you will be able to keep as a treasured souvenir or record. It's ideal for specific experiences and projects, such as the first year of your baby's life, the early years of a relationship, your time at university or college, or your memories and experiences in a particular place. Or it can be a treasured family scrapbook. If you create the journal online then you can include photos, video and music clips. If you create it in a beautiful hardback book or photo album you can include printed memorabilia, photos, handwriting and artwork and you can incorporate scrapbooking techniques so that each page expresses the themes in a variety of ways, and it's very inviting to pick up and browse.

Some legacy journal and memoir prompts

- Introduction: Is this a memoir (a record of part of your life or certain themes in your life) or an autobiography (your complete overall story from birth)?

- What you would like this memoir to include? Who you are hoping will read it? Who are your readers — or is this going to be a private document? What are your intentions for writing it? What would you like to achieve by writing this memoir? What do you hope your readers will take from it? How would you like writing this memoir to change you, and change your readers?

- Background: your ancestry and what you know of your family history; stories and traditions that have come down through the family; how history and social conditions affected and shaped your family over time. What are some of the family themes you can identify that are still present in the current generations, and how are they playing out? What is the relationship between the past and the present that you have experienced in your own life?

- How have your early experiences shaped you? What are the similarities between who you were as a young child, and how you are now? What are some of the things that are still important to you now that were important then?

- What was your experience of childhood and your teenage years? What are the parallels and differences, both in your life now, and with the young people you know today?

- Tell the story of your experience with education, work, career and achievement. How do you feel about this now, compared to when you started out? What would you tell your younger self now, if you could?

- What do you feel are your most significant achievements, ones that are unique to you in your family?

- Tell the story of the social, historical and economic context of your life and times. How has this affected your sense of self and how you think of and describe yourself?

- What do you feel have been your most significant achievements?

- Tell the story of your most important relationships, perhaps beginning with your parents or early carers, siblings and other significant family members you spent time with. Describe how it felt to be with these people by describing the physical locations, the atmosphere, what they looked like, and write out any conversations you can remember. The more specific and relevant descriptive, physical details you can include, the more real and vivid your story can become. See if you can bring these people to life on the page by bringing enough true detail, but not so much information that it might overwhelm a reader and cause them to lose focus.

NOTES

....

....

....

....

....

....

....

....

....

....

....

PART 4

The benefits of journalling

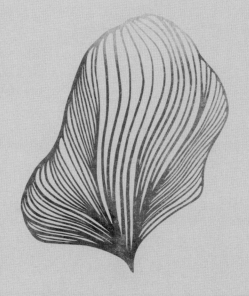

Mindfulness is easier with journalling
because they are made for each other. Your
thoughts no longer go round and round
in your head and you are free to connect
wholeheartedly with whatever inspires you.

CHAPTER 7

Mindfulness and journalling

Journal writing is the practice of mindfulness in action. Journal writing can be a living application of time-honoured mindfulness principles, enabling you to enjoy the benefits of mindfulness while you are doing something you enjoy. Journal writing is a practice, as is meditation, yoga or martial arts — it's not something you do a few times or that you ever get perfect. Journal writing is a lifegiving process that helps you capture and articulate today's tasks and problems, and also today's special mood and magic. It helps you lasso those butterfly thoughts that are so tantalizing. Journal writing is a practice because you are simply required to show up, sit down and pay attention. It's regular and repetitive, both soothing and empowering. It's a form of self-development and self-education. It helps you get everything in life done in a more coherent way. It helps you get out of those circles that go round and round in your head.

Back in 1986 when Natalie Goldberg wrote *Writing Down the Bones*, which has remained a classic popular text on personal journalling, she was a Zen meditation practitioner, and learnt to make writing her practice. She found writing was 'a way to penetrate your life and become sane'. She encouraged her students to 'write down the bones … the essential, awake speech of their minds.'

THE CORE COMPONENTS OF MINDFULNESS IN JOURNAL WRITING

Respect for yourself, for your work and for the world around you is key. This is an attitude that can help you begin, holding an open mind that is respectful of yourself, how you feel, and the dilemmas and choices you face.

Your journalling is also a form of open enquiry. It is an investigation into your own capacities and potential. This is always fresh and unfolding. Your sense of meaning and purpose can deepen and become more enlivened. By showing up and writing in your journal, you respect your process through witnessing and recording it without judgment or criticism, but with openness and receptivity. Some of what you write will simply serve the purpose of clearing your mental and emotional space. If you have ever attended a meditation retreat, you know how much time you spend in conflict and agitation with yourself while you are trying to sit quietly and be peaceful! Yet when you return home, you feel different. You are refreshed and you see yourself and your life from a different perspective. This type of journalling is about self-renewal and there is a little Zen in it.

Don't listen to anyone who tells you that spending time writing about yourself in your journal is self-indulgent, selfish or weird — such people might even feel threatened by your journal habit, or think that you are writing about them. When you start to think about things more clearly, this will bring positive change. Personal and professional growth occur when you take yourself seriously and listen in to what you really want. Then you can act on it. For example, you might get the feeling — just a little nudge — that you need to have more fun and lightness in your life. So write about it, explore it and then follow it up with action, by deliberately doing something fun and enjoyable.

Being present with a feeling, a problem or an attitude means focusing your attention on it. Journalling enables you to bring heightened *awareness* to situations, thoughts or feelings. Awareness is of itself transformative, and this is the whole essence of mindfulness practice. With journal-based mindfulness, the practice is sitting and writing, and rather than sitting and watching your thoughts and feelings go round, you're writing them down. When you write them down, you can let them go and then do something to change your external world to match the changes you are making more subtly in your internal world.

At their heart, all mindfulness traditions can be described as a dialogue between form and emptiness. We are in a continual process of negotiation about how we bring ourselves into form in the world in ways that are happy and productive. Journalling helps bring more clarity and ease to this eternal dance.

Journalling is a life-giving process of capturing today's unique thoughts, the mood and magic of the moment. Regular, mindfulness-based journal writing helps you capture passing thoughts and bright ideas and secure them into a healthy, vital framework where, over time, everything comes together and makes more sense.

A central motif within the various schools of mindfulness is that of the lotus flower. The lotus, a large and beautiful flower similar to a water lily, is celebrated as a symbol of purity and enlightenment. However, the beautiful petals of this flower emerge from muddy water. It needs the nutrition in the mud, and it would not grow in a clear pond of sterile perfection. This is a perfect metaphor for how the daily stuff of our lives, the silt stirred up from the bottom of the pond, is always the real material we work with, and we do not ever need it to be perfect. We need the silt, the grit, the difficult bits to help us see and define more clearly what we value, aspire to, find beautiful and worth working for.

Through mindful, reflective, contemplative writing we can cultivate 'witness consciousness' or the witness self. This is a way of learning to view yourself with detachment. Although you have feelings, sensations and thoughts, these are understood to be the objects of awareness, but they are not the awareness itself. In all forms of mindfulness practice you are encouraged to let go of identifying with the contents of your consciousness, and instead rest in pure awareness, your essential nature, or your self.

Write about things that help you feel centred and peaceful, and focus your attention on enhancing these fundamental qualities of consciousness. Bring attention to the states of being emphasized in the mindfulness traditions, which include compassion for self and others, joy in the wellbeing and good fortune of others, loving kindness and heart-centred action. Acceptance, both self-acceptance and acceptance of others, is central. This is not a passive acceptance of the inevitable or of things such as injustices that need to be changed, but comes from a whole and balanced place when taking action, that is not fuelled by negative feelings or prejudice that are out of awareness. In the mindfulness traditions, core positive states of mind are understood as resource states which are available to everyone, and which can be cultivated further through intentional practice. Cultivating these qualities raises your level of awareness and the positive energy you radiate. For example, reflect upon ways in which you could be kinder, more compassionate and more self-accepting towards yourself.

HOW TO BE A MINDFUL JOURNAL WRITER

A period of intensive focus can be the most important part of your day. Your focus and energy are best in the morning, so if possible write then. If mornings do not work for you, do it whenever you want. There is a short window of opportunity for a few minutes after you wake up, and before you remember what you were preoccupied with yesterday, when you can be in charge and set the tone for the day before things happen that grab your attention.

Give complete attention to your journalling session, and do not do anything else at the same time. Set up your space the day before so it is ordered, clean, pleasant and harmonious, and use a pen and notebook that feel special. Schedule uninterrupted writing sessions, perhaps 15 minutes a day. The environment matters. It needs to be simple and not distracting, without devices or background noise. Each journal session builds on the last and is a practice session rather than an end result, but the repetition of practice sessions builds momentum. Mindfulness supports the simplicity of being present, here and now, and choosing where to place your focus. Being present to, and with, yourself is difficult and if you are easily distracted by stress, anxiety, random mental activity and multitasking, then training your mind to be centred and serene for a few minutes a day is a challenge.

Begin by becoming relaxed, centred and grounded in your body. Begin with a short meditation session, some mindful breathing or a body scan. For now, all you have to focus on is being here, writing. Allow yourself to relax, let go and stop holding onto any particular thoughts or preoccupations. Do not pay attention to the various thoughts and ideas that come to you that suggest you need to be doing something else right now! You want your mind to flow naturally into the physical experience of writing, feeling the pen in your hand and seeing your words flow onto the paper. Hold an attitude of positivity and hopefulness towards your journal, and gratitude for this opportunity.

Your journalling is a form of self-enquiry, an investigation into your own capacities and potential. If it is real and honest, it will always be unfolding on the new wave of your growth and discovery. Your sense of self-authorship, meaning and purpose will keep opening up.

Shrill, till the comrade of his chambers
  woke,
And came upon him half-arisen from
  sleep,
With a weird bright eye, sweating and
  trembling,
His hair as it were crackling into flames,
His body half flung forward in pur-
  suit,
And his long arms stretch'd as to grasp
  a flyer:
Nor knew he wherefore he had made
  the cry;
And being much befool'd and ...
  oted
By the rough amity of the other,
  sank
As into sleep again. The second day,
My lady's Indian kinsman rushing in,
A breaker of the bitter news from
  home,
Found a dead man, a letter edged
  with death
Beside him, and the ... which ...
  himself
Gave Edith, ... and it's
  blood;
'From Edith ...
  blade.
Then Averil ...
  his death
And when he ...
  lieved
Beholding how ...
  not Time's
Had blasted him — ...
  sand days
... ere clipt by horror ...
  life.
Yet the sad mo ...
  death
Scarce touch'd her thro' that nearness
  of the first,
And being used to find her pastor ...
  texts,
Sent to the harrow'd brother, praying
  him
To speak before the people of her child,
And fixt the Sabbath. Darkly that
  day rose,
Autumn's mock sunshine of the faded
  woods
Was all the life of it; for hard on these,
A breathless burthen of low-folded
  heavens

Stifl... ; but every
Sent... ny too had
Ed... ound, and
T... the hapless
... dely mur...
Th... plain-faced
... urning these,
... em, ribbon,
... ch, — one
For green... ings thro' the
  lan...s, —
Still pale, the pale head of him, who
  tow... r'd
Above th... m, with his hopes in either
  gri... e.
Long ... r his bent brows linger'd
  Averill,
His face... magnetic to the hand from
  w... ch
... vid he pluck'd it forth, and labor'd
  th...
His brie... prayer-prelude, gave the
  ve... e, 'Behold,
... our ho... e is left unto you desolate!'
... into so long a pause again
... alf ... azed, half frighted, all his
  floo...
... from his height and loneliness of
  gri...
... down in flood, and dash'd his
  ang... heart
Against th... desolations of the world.

Never s... ce our bad earth became
  one... a,
Which rol... g o'er the palaces of the
  pro...
... nd all bu... hose who knew the living
  God...
E... t that ... ere left to make a purer
  worl...
Wh... since... ad flood, fire, earthquake,
... hu... er, wrought
Such ... ast... and havoc as the idola...
Which ... the low light of mortality

MINDFULNESS JOURNALLING:
A QUICK SUMMARY

- Reduce stress through the soothing, balancing habit of regular mindfulness journalling. When you are more relaxed, everything in life flows more easily.

- Increase your productivity and your results through your focused attention. Your focus, energy and willpower are incredibly powerful when you align them to your chosen goals or purpose. Self-awareness is transformative in and of itself, and by bringing neutral, accepting awareness about who you are on the page, you can have a powerful impact on your own relationship to the subject you are writing about.

- Use a mindfulness approach combined with bullet journalling to monitor habits and behaviours you want to change or develop. A process of regular mindful monitoring can enable you to create new habits or change old ones, through a simple process of daily recording.

- You can apply mindfulness principles to any journal, or you may want to keep a dedicated mindfulness journal, for example when you are learning to become more present and less anxious, solve a particular problem, manage pain, deepen your capacity to be present in your writing, enhance your spiritual practice, or deepen your inquiry into what it is you really truly want.

Mindfulness journalling prompts

There are pre-printed 'mindfulness journal' books available if you would like to follow guided writing prompts each day, but you can easily make your own, or add a mindfulness element to any type of journal. In mindfulness writing sessions the topic you are writing about can be very simple. The purpose of a simple writing prompt is to practise focusing your attention. When you get distracted by other thoughts, gently pull your attention back.

Focus on feelings, situations or worries that you want to change. Describe the situation and what you feel and think about it, and why.

- I feel:

- I think:

- How I see the situation/problem is:

- How my perception of the situation is likely to affect the outcome:

- What I would like to feel better about:

- What I really want in this situation is:

- Use language that is emotionally neutral, in that you are just observing the situation. You are not trying to fix things; you are just bringing a heightened awareness to what is taking place.

- Describe your feelings, thoughts and immediate situation. Use descriptive yet emotionally neutral language and include details such as what you see and feel, so you attend to both what is around you and what is within you.

- Write about yourself in the third person to enhance your ability to observe yourself as a witness. Do not identify with your feelings and thoughts. Write 'I am aware she has a headache and feels tired' rather than 'I have a headache and I feel tired'.

- Journal about your physical and/or emotional pain and discomfort. In mindfulness theory and practice, it is understood that when we are in pain we suffer, but pain and suffering are not regarded as the same. It is what we do with pain, arousal or stress that makes things worse and causes suffering. In pain management clinics, patients have been able to reduce the levels of pain they report by learning to describe the pain in a more detached way. You can keep thinking 'my ankle really hurts now that I have sprained it and I am so worried now I won't be able to work'. Or you can write about it in your journal. Write your close observations of the pain, without minimizing it, catastrophizing it or trying to make it go away; just observe and describe it as an accepting observer. You will find that your resistance to the pain — trying to fight it — tends to make it worse, whereas if you can observe it in a detached, descriptive way, paying close attention to all of its features, it becomes easier to manage. This is only recommended for mild to moderate pain; for severe pain, as for any serious injury, you need to seek professional medical help.

- Use a mindfulness approach to problem solving. Describe the problem, bringing benevolent and kind attention to all aspects of the situation. Allow yourself to be relaxed and comfortable while writing. Bring focused awareness to the problem, without trying to fix it. Just describe it as it is. Leave the journal entry for a few days, then come back and formulate your approach to dealing with the situation based upon the enhanced awareness you have now developed.

- For maximum effectiveness in mindfulness journalling, take a minimalist approach to your subject matter. Write about a narrow range of topics but explore them in depth, and persist with them over time. Be courageous and take risks to go into territory that may be unknown or unexplored about your topic. Look at it from angles you may not have considered previously.

Express how you feel — a simple way
to reduce stress and increase your sense
of wellbeing.

CHAPTER 8

Develop your emotional intelligence with journalling

Emotional intelligence is a profound aspect of intelligence that is not measured by IQ tests but which significantly affects our behaviour, relationships, and how we manage our emotions. The idea of emotional intelligence was popularized in Daniel Goleman's influential book, *Emotional Intelligence*. It can be defined as the ability to understand and influence our own emotions and those of others. Emotional intelligence — our EQ — affects our ability to make decisions, identify opportunities, enjoy relationships and feel confident and self-assured.

Perhaps the most important aspect of EQ is empathy, the ability to recognize — and respond appropriately to — what another person is feeling. There are two types of empathy: how another person's feelings make you feel, and what you understand when witnessing another's feelings, or the ability to analyze and draw conclusions about your observations of what someone is feeling. Empathy can be deepened by anyone using journalling methods, including people who do not have a high level of natural empathy.

EMOTIONAL INTELLIGENCE IS A FOUNDATION OF SUCCESS

Understanding your own emotions, and your emotional reaction to others or to certain situations, is a foundation of good relationships and successful interpersonal skills. Leadership qualities include self-awareness, self-knowledge and self-understanding, and being able to make good use of interpersonal feedback — all qualities that you can deepen by reflecting upon interactions you have witnessed or participated in. Curiosity is another aspect of intelligence: being interested in your own and others' emotional worlds, and taking time to learn about them.

SPECIFIC QUALITIES OF EMOTIONAL INTELLIGENCE

Faith and trust in yourself and others is one of the qualities of emotional intelligence. When you interact with someone who is open, trusting, sincere and secure in themselves, the quality of the interaction is more likely to be easy, stress-free and enjoyable. They do not enact their insecurities and fears upon you, or blame you for the way they are feeling. This faith and loyalty to yourself and to what is important to you is developed by self-awareness and understanding of your priorities, your values, what you are most interested in and what really motivates you.

Holding a positive attitude is an important component of EQ, as success stems from self-belief, happiness, enjoyment, commitment, passion and purpose.

Being flexible and adaptable is another important quality of EQ — understanding when something isn't working, and being able to change course is a signature strength of emotionally intelligent people, as is the ability to recognize opportunities. Those who are emotionally intelligent are not afraid to 'think' with heart and intuition as well as head, and will not do something if it is logically correct yet does not feel right, or would mean harming others. 'Living from the heart' is not an airy romantic fantasy, but a real way to be balanced, centred, harmonious and happy. Intelligent interconnectivity means feeling connected to others as a baseline, rather than feeling separate and that only your individual needs matter.

Emotional intelligence journalling prompts

Write down your observations of other people's emotions, and reflect upon them. Think about how you would want to be treated if it was you who felt that way. Take time to explore emotions that do not completely make sense to you, and come to an understanding of why the person feels the way they do.

Write detailed observations of people who appear to be emotionally intelligent and who have positive relationships, good conversations or great interpersonal skills in the workplace. Observe carefully and reflect upon what they say and do that works so well. When you have the opportunity, use some of these approaches in your own conversations, and again record and reflect upon the results.

Explore how you habitually manage your emotions. Identify them, name them, record them, express them, explore them, and come to understand them more fully. Learn to distinguish the different nuances of emotions; for example, irritation, aggravation, annoyance, rage and fury are all completely different.

Explore your own emotional wellbeing. Write observations of how you feel each day, and especially what works in nudging you towards consistent positivity.

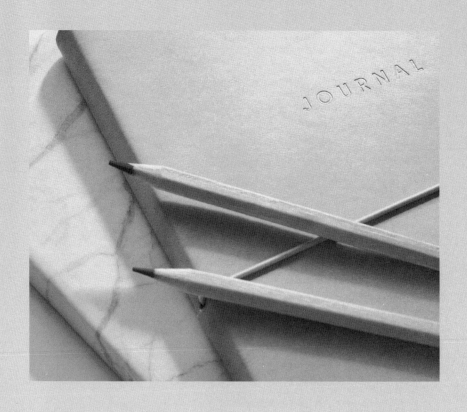

Look back on where you are now from the future, where your current problems have been resolved and forgotten. You can change anything if you journal yourself into the right mindset.

CHAPTER 9

Therapeutic journalling

Many different studies undertaken by research psychologists have indicated positive outcomes when people write for the purpose of increasing their wellbeing. There are a lot of these studies because journal writing is a relatively easy topic to research. For the same reasons, journalling can be of benefit to you personally — it is accessible, free, and you can easily assess and finetune the results for yourself.

Psychotherapy and counselling encourage you to become more compassionate towards yourself, to develop greater self-insight, and to focus on developing positive feelings and achievements. The intention of a therapeutic journal is to help you develop these results over time, independently of seeing a therapist. Who could not benefit from developing a more positive focus, greater self-understanding and appreciation, and more constructive habits? You achieve these improvements gradually in small, manageable amounts so that you can install and integrate the improvements in your life.

You have probably heard of the gratitude journal, a journalling technique where you write a daily list of things you are grateful for. You write 'I am grateful for … my lovely cup of coffee/my clean laundry/my son being here with me/the lovely music on the radio …' and so on. The purpose is to change your mindset over time, as gratitude as an attitude is a direct antidote to fear, worry, self-doubt and negativity. The simple action of turning your attention to gratitude for ordinary things in your daily existence helps you change your focus. Many therapeutic approaches to journalling — and the reported therapeutic effect of maintaining a journal output over time — rely on quite simple techniques for changing your mindset. You can't change the things that happened that have made you feel miserable, or less effective than you would like to be, but you can change your attitude to them, and you can learn a constructive approach to problem-solving and meeting challenges so that you can move forward in a completely different way.

The gratitude journal is a form that has received quite a lot of attention from psychology researchers, and staff at the University of Montana who conducted a review of available research concluded that the research really is positive. There is a direct correlation between expressing gratitude and many documented aspects of good physical and psychological wellbeing. To express this simply: it cheers you up. In addition to posting gratitude entries in a journal, Martin Seligman at the University of Pennsylvania (known for his work on emotional resilience and positive psychology) asked his team to research the results of people calling or writing someone to directly express their gratitude in person. Both those who communicated the gratitude, and those who received it, reported positive outcomes, such as feeling more productive and having higher levels of self-worth. So it seems important that the gratitude habit you develop in your journal does not just stay in your journal, but that you occasionally send a thank you letter or make a call. This has developed further into the concept of 'happy mail' where people send each other lovely and uplifting surprises by snail mail.

A refinement of the gratitude journal is the celebrations journal. In this journal, you begin and end each day by writing down things you enjoy, celebrate or appreciate, both past and present. This can be about positive memories and experiences from any time in your life, whether today or many years ago. If you do not feel there is anything to celebrate about today, you write about a pleasant memory. This type of journalling has been shown to have a sustained positive effect on your sense of wellbeing and helps you entrain with positive memories and positive experiences.

VIBRANT LISTS

Use a simple yet effective journalling technique to help you spend as much of your day as possible in your zone of being happy, bright, productive and focused. This only takes a few minutes and is best done early in the morning.

Begin your day by writing lists of what you are going to do today, and what you intend to feel and achieve today. This is not your usual to-do list, but is all about helping you feel more upbeat, empowered and effective by training your attention on positive feelings. Try this for yourself to discover the difference it can make to your day. When you feel more positive, you are more fully aligned with your sense of flow. When you are in your flow, everything comes together and works out more easily. A regular journalling practice is necessary to help you stay focused on your positive intentions, as it is so easy to be distracted. If you find that at some point in the day you have lost your focus, go back to the journal and review what you wrote, and perhaps refocus your intentions for the rest of the day, and for getting through whatever has come up. This means that when problems and issues arise in the day that throw you off course, you don't just cope with them as best you can. Remember your journal and re-orient yourself to today's intentions. What is the most positive and constructive way of getting through this for yourself and all concerned? What's the most important focus to hold on to? Breathe, relax and become centred for just a few moments. Try to gain a little perspective by imagining you are looking back at this day from five years in the future. What's most important? How do you want to appear to the world in the light of history and hindsight?

Writing prompts
for your vibrant lists

Focus on what I want and intend to feel today:

- The mindset I want to establish and maintain today.

- What am I going to focus on to bring a feeling of excitement and fulfilment to today?

- What are the good things I am looking forward to today?

- What is around me that I can enjoy, celebrate and appreciate today?

Set reminders for the mindset, feelings, tone and mood I want to maintain throughout today's activities (for example, when I am in the dentist's chair I intend to feel cheerful and relaxed).

'DEAR DIARY': THE BENEFITS OF A THERAPEUTIC STYLE OF JOURNALLING

There are many benefits from keeping a journal that apply to everyone, not just to those of us with identifiable difficulties such as low confidence or depression. Writing about your day, your concerns and your feelings can help you relax, help you solve problems more effectively, and park them. If you find yourself waking up in the night, keep a journal by your bedside and write down whatever is on your mind.

Writing down your problems and concerns helps you to express your feelings and organize your thoughts better and this can benefit your physical health, as well as your memory recall in later life. For example, a study was carried out at the University of Arizona where people who had been through divorce journalled about their stressful divorce experiences. This helped the participants to process the emotional rollercoaster they had been on, and they felt better equipped to move on — interestingly, they showed lower heart rates and heart rate variability.[1]

Writing about personal and relationship issues is much cheaper than seeing a therapist but it can take just as much time, and you need to set yourself clear agendas and tasks so that you actively work to feel better. Writing about your negative feelings could in some situations make you feel worse, so it is not advisable to engage in long writing sessions about negative feelings without support and a clear structure and intentions for what the writing is for.

Therapeutic journalling prompts

These are just examples to inspire you, as you will be able to devise prompts that are perfect for you and your individual situation.

- Write a one-sentence journal entry at the end of the day, summarizing the important moments of the day.

- Explore one current, ongoing aspect of life, such as a relationship, a job or your parenting skills. Add comments, thoughts and reflections over time. On different days, you will have different perspectives, but keep returning to the topic as new material arises in daily life. This will help you bring reflective self-awareness to the situation, and after a while you may find yourself acting more mindfully and skilfully without working on it too hard or even discussing any of it with the other people involved.

- Write down, under organized headings, everything that is bothering you about one specific situation, for example, list the facts, your worries and concerns, your questions, specifically what you need to resolve, and the timing. Then write the answer to this question: How would you feel if this problem/situation was resolved in the most benevolent way possible? Describe how you would feel, and how it would all look if this was no longer a problem. Then close the journal and leave it at least overnight, and if possible for a few days. When you go back to it, read over what you wrote, then write yourself a timed plan of action to actively support the best possible results you can hope for. Follow up the actions according to the timing, and report back on your ongoing progress. If new consequences emerge, then journal them too.

- Deal with any procrastination that is bugging you by taking a different approach. Write about what life would be like if you never did the thing you are supposed to. How does it feel if you let yourself off the hook? Or how would it be if you only did it when you felt like it?

- Be a witness to your everyday moments. Every day has different qualities and it is a unique day for you on planet Earth! At the end of the day, recall a few moments. Write in an accepting style, without any self-criticism or judgments.

- Celebrate all the things you did today, and the personal qualities, skills and strengths you applied and demonstrated today.

- Write a confidence-building journal. Identify a few areas where you work on developing your confidence and set yourself small, manageable targets and 'action experiments' to gradually develop more confidence. For example, if you feel underconfident about your ability to socialize, make dates for events to go to and make the effort to meet people and start a conversation with them. Report back to your journal about how it went and adjust your targets as you go. Give yourself praise and feedback on how your action experiments worked out.

PROCESSING THE PAST

Journalling offers a fantastic opportunity to address issues, 'stuff', 'emotional baggage', emotional history, negative self-beliefs and poor self-esteem. It's an opportunity to challenge and work through anything that makes you feel negative or miserable about yourself, and any attitudes, beliefs or self-talk that make you feel less than good enough. There is no time like now to learn to value yourself and treat yourself right. There is no reason why you need to continue in life with repeating emotional problems or cycles of the same old negative relationships. Journalling offers you an incredible resource for change, and all you need is some patience, persistence and structure.

In working with the past, mine your experience for what you want to keep and what you no longer need. Wisdom comprises the learning that you are able to extract from your life experience, how you apply it in the now, and how you are able to pass on these benefits to others. So first of all you can identify the areas of your past that you would like to learn from, grow from and move on from.

It can be empowering to see the connection between past experiences and how they informed your current reality, and the choices you continue to make that are still influenced by the past. When you stop to take a look at this, it is like pressing a big pause button. You become more aware of how the past lives on in the present, and through this raised awareness you become much more aware of any ways in which you may be repeating the past. For example, imagine that you were influenced by a mother who was successful and career-focused, and when you were fourteen she took a job that meant she worked long hours. You felt envious of your friends at school who had mothers who were always there when they came home, whereas you felt quite lonely letting yourself into an empty house every day after school. You now insist on being home for your own children and pass up any job opportunities that might mean working later, even though your children are old enough and do not seem to mind whether you are home or not. Now that they are secure and confident young people, you could branch out more in your choice of work — but you use the fact that the children need you at home as an excuse for your lack of confidence. This is a simple example of something from the past that is being perpetuated, that is out of date because it has not been consciously examined. You can use your journal to freshen up your life and bring yourself up to date, so that there are fewer areas in life where you do things the way you've always done them, simply because you have never thought it through.

With any personal issue that needs resolution, it's helpful to have a sense of where it started, how this informed where you are, and where you truly want to go next.

WRITING IN THE AFTERMATH OF TRAUMA AND ABUSE

If you have experienced trauma, abuse, traumatic displacement or loss, or traumatic stress disorder, it is important to find ways to process these experiences so that you can still enjoy life. However, just writing a narrative account of what happened, or just telling someone what happened, is often not therapeutic or helpful in itself. In fact, it can re-traumatize you, as part of your brain cannot tell the difference between the past and the present and you can re-experience the trauma happening all over again every time you repeat it. So, telling the story of what happened is not, by itself, therapeutic and it may even reinforce the vortex of the trauma and keep you cycling around it. Thus, your writing needs to have clear intentions and a clear structure.

If you write to express and release your feelings, then review how you feel during and after the writing and evaluate whether this writing is helping you feel better.

One of the ways in which your experiences may have been very difficult to process and recover from is that perhaps you felt disempowered, helpless or victimized. Perhaps you dissociated, froze or lost some memories. You can use the writing process to help you overcome the syndrome of 'learned helplessness' that sometimes happens when you have experienced situations that were beyond your control. This can happen to anyone, but particularly when you lose awareness during or after the event/s. It means that combinations of ordinary, everyday events can sometimes trigger you to re-enact aspects of what happened, or you become fearful or have a panic attack.

Writing your story in a more active and empowered way can help you feel more fully engaged in life again. This means you take charge of the story and write it from your own viewpoint, as the author of your own experience. As the author, you are in charge of the ending, which means you are free to choose the attitude and approach you now want to take, both towards yourself and the people who were involved in this. The bad guys have only won if you do not recover. Perhaps you have valuable learning that you would like to share with others facing similar circumstances? Perhaps you would like to write down how you now feel towards people who hurt you? So, be sure to include your comments and thoughts in your writing, and do not just tell what happened. Give your work a title, subheadings, structure and direction, with a beginning, a middle and an end. In your conclusion, gather together the important things you have discovered and learned and how you would like to take these forward in your next steps in life. Perhaps you can make a plan so this no longer affects you in the same way. Establish a sense of closure and moving on.

Prompts for writing about personal history

- Give yourself themes or topics to write about, and stick to them so you don't start writing about 'everything' in a big blob! Break things down into small, manageable topics. Go into detail about just a few topics, rather than writing generally about a lot of topics. Topics could include, for example, your earliest memories, your relationship with a pet, the landscapes or cities where you have lived, memories of family members, the things that inspired and excited you when you were young, and the things you wanted to do 'when you grew up'. Use dates and headings for your entries so that you can find them again.

- Write letters to your future selves, say in five, ten and fifteen years' time.

- Write letters to your children and loved ones that you would like them to read when you are gone.

- Write letters to anyone, such as a public figure, a grandparent, an ancestor or even an abstract entity, which you will not post, but which give you the opportunity to express something unique and special that is evoked in your relationship with this person.

JOURNAL WRITING AS AN ADJUNCT TO THERAPY OR COUNSELLING

While you are attending therapy or counselling, you can get much more out of it, and save yourself time and money, by speeding up your therapeutic progress in your journal. Some therapists and counsellors may be interested in your journal or encourage you to use it for homework assignments, and some do not work in this way — but you can do it anyway. You can attain your desired changes and results in your life much more quickly if you take a proactive approach. For example, journal about your goals in therapy — these can change as you move through it — so you and your therapist work together in a co-creative partnership and stay on the same page. Write down any important insights or experiences that emerge during the therapeutic hour, as you can easily forget them. One of the key differences in how therapy works much better for some people than others is in how they actively apply the therapy in everyday life. If you enjoy your discussions in therapy but then forget all about it till next week, it will take much longer than if you process your therapeutic work in your journal and focus on the positive changes you intend to put into practice. After all, the important work takes place in your life.

WORKING WITH YOUR RESISTANCE TO CHANGE

It may not be helpful to be too analytical in your journal, to become too logical or to look at the causes behind your symptoms or feelings. Too much of this kind of analysis does not help you change and can even further reinforce your old ways of thinking! It is one way in which you could become caught up in resistance and defences, and slow down your process. If you find yourself getting tangled up in negative thinking in your journal it is best to leave it and try a different approach.

When you are working on yourself, you have to tread a line between experiencing your more difficult feelings and symptoms and offering them kindness, understanding and acceptance, and moving on from them in constructive ways. At some time during this change process, everyone experiences some resistance, as there is in all of us a strong pull to maintain the status quo, which has kept us 'safe' in the past.

When this 'stay the same and stay safe' part of you is stimulated and challenged by therapy, you could regress to where you started, decide that therapy is pointless, engage in risk-taking behaviour or go back on resolutions you've made. When this more destructive part of you comes forward, it is a good sign that the therapy is reaching you in the right places, even though this is the exact time that many people decide they do not need therapy anymore! It's very helpful if you can be a little detached from the resistance and continue your journalling as normal. Just write about your resistance as an aspect of yourself in a calm and accepting way. Help yourself see clearly what you are doing, and reframe your focus. Learning and growth always involve stepping backwards as well as forwards, as change doesn't happen in a linear way. It can be visualized more as a spiral process, with big leaps forward that are suddenly interrupted when you hit an old trigger and you feel as if you have gone back to the old you.

Journalling prompts to help tackle resistance to change

- Identify the methods of resistance you commonly use, such as procrastination, avoidance, forgetting, distraction or making excuses, and write them out. Being aware of them is the first step.

- Journal whenever you are confused or experiencing self-doubt, so that you can feel centred and clear, so you can reconnect with your coherence.

- If you tackle resistance head on it can really kick back, so often a soft approach works better. Give your resistance a name and have a written dialogue or conversation with him or her in your journal. Ask him or her what she/he needs from you, and ask them to leave you alone!

- Each week, push yourself to do something new or different that is outside your comfort zone and journal about the process.

- Build up momentum for change so that it becomes both enjoyable and inevitable. Plan and review this process regularly.

Journalling prompts to help you get the most from therapy

- When writing a therapy journal include both your feelings and your thoughts, as engaging your authentic feelings is an essential component of real and lasting change.

- Define your aims and intentions for therapy. State specifically what you want from it and the changes you want to make. How will your life feel and look when these intended outcomes have been achieved? Ensure that you and your therapist reach agreement on what these outcomes are to be, as they need to stretch you, yet be realistic and achievable over time.

- Work on one topic at a time, and don't mix them up. Even if you feel you have many different things you need to work on, you will be overwhelmed if you try to do them all at once. Work on one topic per week, and don't go on to the next until you have recorded positive changes you are happy with. This is because you can transfer successful learning from one area to another.

- How can you help bring the feeling of these desired outcomes forward into your life, perhaps through small daily changes that you can make? Record these changes and the results you experience, for example diarize a situation in which you challenged your habitual anxiety and did something new and different.

- Reflect on what was discussed, any processes you went through, and how it all made you feel, as soon as possible after each session. Note down any questions or concerns you still have so you can bring them back to the therapist next time.

- Summarize the insights, learning, the recognition and the 'aha' moments — these arise spontaneously in the therapeutic encounter. They are precious, but they are so easy to forget.

- Write down a situation, or a few situations, where you will attempt to apply new insights or strategies this week. Keep an ongoing record of how it goes, and what you learn or what questions come up for you during the week.

IDENTIFY YOUR 'LIFE STATEMENTS'

Life statements are a kind of decision we make when we are young, usually before the age of fourteen or so, when we decide to take a certain approach to situations based upon our perception of our life experience. We then apply this, unconsciously, later in life even in situations where the life statement has lost its relevance, but we still cling on to it.

Life statements are generally erroneous premises upon which we base a lifetime of behaviour.

An example would be if your father spoke to you in a way that made you feel diminished and unvalued. Your life statement might be, 'Older men never respect me and I will never respect them, either'. You then subconsciously believe that the men closest to you don't respect you, and you see their attitude towards you as lacking in respect. In turn, you behave in an angry or defensive way towards them, or are generally prickly or awkward with them. A life statement is a lens that you see through, rather than an objective reality, and it takes careful work to identify your life statements. Once you become aware of them, you can begin to change them, but of course you cannot change anything before you are aware of what it is. A key to identifying life statements is to look out for any area in life where you have persistent patterns of feelings, thoughts or behaviour that are not productive, that have perhaps repeated over many years or that make it difficult for people to be around you.

Record any dreams you remember by writing them down when you wake up. Some of your dreams will be directly relevant and some not, but you won't know till later. Often dreams don't make sense at the time but later on you can see that some of them have an interesting meaning relating to your therapy.

Work intensively on patterns that you want to change, by closely recording:

- the event that triggered the unwanted feelings or behaviour
- the thoughts and feelings that led up to the event, the behaviour and the feelings
- the thoughts and feelings you experienced during and immediately after the event
- why you had these thoughts and feelings — what was it about this event that triggered them?
- the beliefs and assumptions you need to change in order to set up more positive and constructive situations in future.

When you gather all of this information together, you can see the underlying beliefs that keep outdated patterns running. Awareness brings in fresh air, and once you can see what is going on in your mind, it no longer holds power over you — you can see how you are doing it to yourself. Once you see this, you have the key to changing anything that you want, one step at a time.

Write down a list of your negative thoughts and concepts about yourself on one side of the page. Write them down quickly and do not dwell on them. On the other side, write the opposite, a statement that is both positive and realistic to correspond with each negative item. For example, if your negative item is 'everyone thinks I am boring', your positive statement is 'I'm really interested in x and I have lots of amazing ideas to share' or 'I'm lonely' becomes 'I'm finding it much easier to connect with people'.

Use your journal to make changes to your mindset by basing your concepts and beliefs about yourself on modern positive psychology, and not on outdated, deterministic or fatalistic views that make you feel passive and helpless. You can achieve any changes you want by changing your thinking so it replicates the qualities you want in your life. The essence of success is believing in yourself, no matter what. This means 'be the change that you want to see' or make your journalling match the way you want your life to be. How you write about yourself helps you redefine who you are and what you can become. So write a list of the qualities and attributes you value about yourself, and write personal bespoke affirmations, for example 'I am happy and it is all working out', 'I am becoming more confident and productive and I've been getting great feedback'.

BE YOUR OWN LIFE OR CAREER COACH WITH JOURNALLING

The process of much life and business coaching follows processes you can easily adapt to journalling, for example:

- Define and describe your current situation to increase your self-awareness.

- Evaluate what is working well and what you need to change.

- Identify and become inspired by a sense of purpose and meaningful goals that express your values.

- Identify and source the information and lifestyle changes you need to put in place, for example education, training, time management, relaxation or exercise.

- Identify your personal fears, self-doubts, resistance, blocks and interpersonal difficulties that create limitations or problems for you, and develop strategies for dealing with them effectively.

- Learn to solve problems and deal with a wide variety of situations flexibly, appropriately and skilfully.

- Put a system of accountability in place to regularly monitor and assess your growth and progress.

While coaches provide excellent techniques, skills and resources to coax, encourage and prod you every step of the way — and may be better than you at identifying your blind spots — you can work through these topics for yourself in a journal, if you are willing to set time aside for this. You can also use journalling alongside coaching to reduce your reliance on the coach or prepare for coaching so you get the most value from it.

You need to build in the accountability and feedback that talking with a coach provides, as well as assignments to undertake each week. Bullet journalling is an excellent resource for self-coaching, and you can use adapted versions of the points above as tasks in your BuJo (refer back to page 79 for bullet journalling details). What you will need to be very aware of is how your resistance to change is playing out. We all have two aspects: the part of us that wants to learn, grow, develop, evolve and embrace change; and the part that will do anything to maintain the status quo and hold off the threat of change by keeping us firmly within our known comfort zone. A coach or therapist is trained to recognize and challenge patterns of resistant behaviour such as avoidance, making excuses, delaying or procrastinating. A coach will move you faster through a process because they will confront and challenge your resistance to change and offer you specific techniques to move through it.

JOURNALLING FOR HAPPY RELATIONSHIPS

A journal can be a great resource to help you maintain and improve your relationship. Here are some relationship journalling prompts for you.

- Write about happy and positive times you have had together. Reminding yourself of all the positive aspects of your relationship helps to reinforce them.

- Each day, write something that you value, love, respect or appreciate about your partner. This writing exercise can literally make you a better person as you focus on the aspects of the other person that you feel aligned. It takes your attention away from those aspects where your partner may not please you.

- Create a list of things to do for your partner to show your love and appreciation and to help him or her feel good. Ensure these are things he or she would like, rather than what you would like.

- Journal about your feelings in the relationship, and what you are learning. Review where you are, and brainstorm some new approaches to any persistent problems.

- What would you like to see more of/less of in the relationship? Write yourself some prompts to help facilitate these changes.

- Are you working through a relationship 'curve' or is it more serious? Write down in detail any stressful events and how you each dealt with them. Record the details of recurring difficulties so you can get them clear in your mind and formulate the best response to them rather than reacting in the moment. Write down how you felt during an argument, and try to understand why you felt this way. Are you overreacting, or was it them?

- Improve on your communication skills. Practise writing skilful and tactful ways to raise issues and bring up your point of view, in a way that is most likely to elicit a positive response.

IS THIS A GOOD RELATIONSHIP? WILL IT LAST?

A question many people ask themselves is whether their relationship is going to last, is it time to make a commitment, should I stay or go — and what is needed is a method to help you evaluate the relationship and its potential staying power. You can both write your answers and then discuss them, as the areas where you see things differently are where you need to work on your communication. When you journal about it, you get to decide whether you want to keep the relationship rather than wondering if it is 'meant to be'.

Here are some things to consider and address as you journal about your relationship.

- What are your expectations of what makes a good relationship? What models of relationship have you absorbed from your family and culture? In what ways is your relationship similar or different from that of both sets of parents?

- Evaluate the quality of your friendship — is this a good friendship? Couples who go the distance tend to be good friends. Describe the relationship as a friendship. Describe instances where the friendship aspect of the relationship was in the foreground. Can you and your partner put the needs of the relationship and the needs of the other person ahead of your own needs, some of the time?

- Are you able to see the best in each other, and support and encourage each other to bring out the best? Do you support each other to do well in life, not just in the relationship?

- Do you both make substantial efforts to make the other person feel valued, loved or appreciated — in ways that are important to the other person, and not just the way you want to do it?

- What is your relationship based upon? Do you want the same things? What is your written or unwritten contract about the purpose of your relationship and the needs you are happy to meet for each other?

- Do you have realistic expectations of what the relationship and your partner can provide? What are your expectations of him or her? Do you know what your partner expects of you?

- Can you engage in open, straight communication? Can you discuss anything with each other? Can you raise issues in a constructive and helpful way, and are they responded to in the spirit of open communication?

- Do you make regular time together to maintain the relationship?

- Can you both work together as a team when there are problems, stressful issues, differences of opinion or different expectations?

- If you want to have children or already have children, are your approaches to parenting compatible?

- Are you both committed to being together and supporting each other when life is difficult?

- Do you each have your own network of family and friends you can rely on?

SINGLE PEOPLE SEEKING A RELATIONSHIP

If you are currently single and would like to be in a relationship, it's a good time for some self-reflective journalling. First you can write about previous relationships and what you have learned from them and how they made you feel, then define and explore your intentions for a new relationship. Write about how you want to feel in your future relationships.

Here are some other points to consider.

- What are some relationship patterns you do not want to repeat? What can you do to ensure you do not find yourself in a 'same old' situation? Do you need to do some work to let go of painful past events or losses?

- Evaluate your 'relationship behaviour' such as your assertiveness, relationship boundaries, communication skills and what presses your buttons. Even just listing these can help you become more self-aware so you can change them.

- What are your expectations and desires for a relationship? And what can you do to realize these in a new relationship?

- Rather than writing a shopping list of the qualities of your ideal partner, write about how you would like to feel in your new relationship. Imagine yourself feeling happy and fulfilled. Describe how this feels, emotionally and physically. Write about this in the present tense, for example describe yourself going to an event together or relaxing together in a garden.

- Now is a good time to set up good self-care habits and track them.

- Work on your self-worth, your confidence and positive self-belief. Write a daily list of a few things you love and appreciate about yourself.

A SIMPLE JOURNAL PROCESS FOR IMPROVING
A STUCK RELATIONSHIP

If you feel your relationship is stuck and would like to change things for the better, consider the points below as you journal about the relationship.

- Define what isn't working, and how you want things to be different.

- Identify the different voices of child and adult within you that play out in the relationship. When are you in child mode and when are you in adult mode? The relationship will work when both of you are in adult mode. What will support you to maintain your adult mode of relating?

- Are you subconsciously operating on negative beliefs based on insecurity, low self-esteem or the examples of your parents? Separate the different layers of beliefs sandwiched together that are making it difficult for you to stay feeling confident as an independent and resourceful adult, for example:

> I want to feel secure and safe, I feel terrified when I feel alone, and I might never find another relationship, and so:

> I have to appease and placate him/her so he or she will stay with me, and I have to accept his/her behaviour even when it upsets me.

- Focus on journalling to increase your confidence and self-esteem, and use mindfulness approaches to help you develop new ways of thinking. You can only change yourself — you cannot change your partner — but you will no longer react in the same way.

JOURNALLING FOR STRESS, ANXIETY OR DEPRESSION

Writing a journal can definitely help with depression, low mood and anxiety. Write it down and let it go — or learn new techniques for nudging yourself towards a more positive attitude.

Set up a journal where you can vent your feelings for a limited time each day. This means you no longer have to ask your friends and family to listen to you, as this can have a negative effect on your relationships. Writing about your negative emotions can improve your mental wellbeing by providing a safe, accepting space where you can really 'hear your own voice'. Self-expression and having a way to release how you feel are really important. You could also consider bringing creative or artistic elements to this, such as expressing some of how you feel in poetry or in drawings, photos, selfies, paintings or collages. Free expression can help you to feel stronger to validate, affirm and express your feelings, and provides release and containment.

Stop ruminating about your worries, and instead write them down, then let them go. Holding on to something by repeatedly thinking about it means you are set in a recurring cycle, so an important aspect of journalling is letting go.

Researchers at Northumbria University found that a sample of normal subjects who were asked to write about positive experiences in their life for 20 minutes a day reported significantly reduced stress and anxiety compared to those who were asked to write about a neutral topic, such as their plans for the day.[2] These benefits also persisted some weeks after the end of the writing exercise, suggesting that this simple approach brought a fundamental change to the way the subjects felt and thought about themselves. These benefits are significant and you can very easily bring them into your own life through journalling.

This has an important implication for journal writing: in order to help yourself feel better, you should make incremental upward adjustments to your mood. It's important to write when you are stressed or in a low mood, but you need to follow some structure. So express and release difficult feelings for up to 20 minutes, then focus on how you would like to feel. Then explore small steps you can take to help yourself feel a little better.

Take as an example the idea that you have decided you wish to lose some weight, and you have been cutting back on calories for a few weeks. One weekend you are at a friend's house celebrating someone's birthday and you are offered lots of wine and cake. Each time you nudge yourself away from the cake, you nudge yourself towards a new version of you who is slimmer and who doesn't need chocolate cake in order to feel good. If you eat more than one piece, you're in effect saying to yourself that the part of you who has always eaten chocolate cake in the past is more powerful than the newer, slimmer version of you who is still developing. So what are your choices in this situation? What would you do?

JOURNALLING FOR WHEN YOU CAN'T SLEEP

If you find yourself awake at night with worries and thoughts going round in your mind, you can break this cycle by writing down in your journal what you are feeling and thinking. Stress and anxiety can be triggered by all kinds of life events, things that everyone experiences, but when you are alone with them at night it's easy to find yourself wide awake. Journalling could also help you fall asleep more easily. A study published in the *Journal of Experimental Psychology* focused on the effects of writing a to-do list for the next day in a journal before going to bed. The result was that the subjects fell asleep nine to ten minutes faster than normal.[3]

If something is really bothering you, you may need to write more than a list. Write the complete story of what you have been going through, including your feelings and thoughts, and anything that has been traumatic for you. By putting this entire situation, event or cluster of feelings down on paper, you are helping your brain to process, integrate and come to terms with what has been happening, so it won't then keep you awake. The writing process will calm you and possibly reduce your heart rate. If this works for you, why not create the habit of organizing your thoughts and feelings in bedtime journalling sessions. Don't be concerned if some nights you find yourself writing some of the same things, and don't in any way judge or evaluate what you write, just take note of how it affects the way you feel.

Journal writing is a premium process
for self-reflective learning, professional
development and self-coaching.

CHAPTER 10

Journalling for academic or professional benefit

A good journal can form the heart of your studies or your continuing professional development. You can use journalling combined with organized note-taking to reinforce good study habits. You can record, process and organize material you are studying and have to write about, such as for a degree, case studies, reports, papers, essays, a thesis or dissertation. If you journal from the beginning of your course, so much the better, but it is never too late to start. Create your own learning journal system that you refine over time.

A NOTE-TAKING SYSTEM

Start with good organization and record your source materials so that they are easy to locate and read back over. This is the basis of beginning to build your own bank of knowledge that you transform into understanding.

By employing a good note-taking system you begin to make the material your own. There is clear evidence that writing by hand has distinct advantages, as people remember material they have handwritten much better than when they have typed it. You also remember more if you draw, alongside or within your text, for example making simple symbols or pictures to convey a concept, so that a meaning is linked to a simple image. The quality of the drawing is unimportant — you could, for example simply draw circles with faces, or basic shapes linked to one another. A study carried out at Waterloo University in Canada found that people could easily recall the meaning of 30 words they had written on a page and linked each of the words to an image, compared with people who had written only the meanings, who could recall some of them but could not recall all of them so easily.[1]

THE CORNELL NOTE-TAKING SYSTEM

Developed at Cornell University in the 1950s, this method of note-taking can help you take notes that are organized, effective and useful.

Here is an adaptation of the Cornell note-taking system you may like to try. Divide the page into three boxes: a narrow box running down the left-hand side; a big one taking up about two-thirds of the page; and a box across the bottom, taking about a third of the page or less. In the main right-hand column, write your in-the-moment notes. Break up the text with dividers, images, doodles, stepped boxes, bulleted lists and customized icons. Use colour, with different pens or highlighters. Include your references here, clearly laid out in the correct format so you can easily find them again. When you have finished, fill in the left-hand column with headings for the key points in the main column. Write these headings in your own words whenever possible. Then in the box at the bottom, write a summary of the most important ideas on this page — just one or two sentences. Again, write this in your own words and images, to make it your own and express it in a way that makes good sense to you; for example, you might connect the most important ideas in linked sub-boxes. When you have finished all the notes on a given topic, go back over them and give the pages overall titles and headings.

When you look back over your notes, whether you are studying for an exam or writing a paper, it will be clear where the most important ideas are. When you write the notes, you may not realize which will be the most important later on, so each page needs a clear title — and ideally put a list of contents at the front of the folder, pad or notebook. Your handwriting does not need to be pretty, just clear; print if your cursive handwriting is hard to read.

SUBJECT	DATE	TOPIC

CUES	NOTES

CUES	NOTES
KEY POINTS MAIN IDEAS	Bulleted List ☐ Thoughts and ideas ☐ main points ☐ diagrams/charts ☐ outlines ☐ leave space between topics

SUMMARY OF THE IMPORTANT NOTES
in your own words, what matters most to you.

FAST

Jim Kwik, a learning coach, uses the acronym FAST in guiding students to become better learners.

- Forget what you think you know already, and just be present and attentive.

- Active: participate actively and stay involved. Don't go into bystander mode if someone is giving a talk or you are reading a book or article — respond to it by writing, scribbling, discussing or putting things into practice.

- State: long-term memory is dependent upon your emotional state, so regulate your emotions so that you feel positive.

- Teach what you have been learning about. One of the best ways of really learning something is to explain it to someone else.

THE REFLECTIVE JOURNAL AS A COURSE REQUIREMENT

Many degrees, courses, training and other programs ask students to keep a reflective journal as a course requirement. This is an invaluable aspect of the transformational learning process. Whether you are a student, a lecturer or trainer, or you manage employees or team members who are engaged in learning, it's useful to understand the intention and value of this resource in depth — it can greatly enhance the learning experience and the student journey. It is an inexpensive resource to utilize with individuals or groups who need to integrate new learning and change, and who may encounter some personal resistance or challenge on the road to change.

Some courses require students to hand in a learning journal as part of an assessment process, and others suggest it as a resource. On some courses, students are not given detailed guidelines about how to leverage the journal writing process to get the most value out of it, and unless the staff actually understand this for themselves, it can be a missed opportunity.

TRACKING YOUR LEARNING

A reflective journal is not a learning log, a course log, a tick-box record of achievements or requirements, a precis of course material, or your course notes or reading notes. These progress-tracking elements are, however, something you may also want to incorporate in a journal that is either separate or adjacent to your reflective learning journal, depending on the individual course requirements. You could, for example, incorporate the course progression elements into a comprehensive study journal that you set up in bullet journal format with all the dates and information you need for your assignments — or there are excellent pre-printed academic planners that you can adapt to help you organize all of this.

It can be empowering to track your progress. Recording both your input and output will help you stay in charge of your learning, meet deadlines without undue stress, and keep all your information organized and accessible. You may have seen students who have not done this, who don't remember when assignments are due or who leave an important course requirement till the last minute. The process of tracking your learning, your input, your output and the timings involved will in itself help you be a more effective and successful learner. Although it will take you time to set it up and review it, this will be time well spent, as the simple actions of observing, recording and reviewing your goals, assignments, deadlines and achievements put you in the driving seat, and heighten your awareness.

REFLECTIVE JOURNALLING AS A TEACHING AND LEARNING STRATEGY

Structured, reflective journalling in response to reading, courses, workshops, seminars, meetings, work placements, problem-solving or internship experience can massively assist your growth and development, cement your skills, and integrate and ground your understanding. Targeted journalling can even help you obtain better grades in your assignments, receive excellent feedback about your progress and development, or increase the impact and value of your contributions. Journalling can help you learn more effectively, by providing you with a space where you can reflect on your learning and realize your stage of development in relation to the desired learning outcomes. Reflective journalling about learning helps you to become more switched on and insightful. Insight is the ability to reflect upon and integrate your learning and experience so that you can apply it. Insight and self-awareness are useful in many different careers, but come as premium in the professions where high quality interpersonal skills are required.

The ability to be self-reflective and self-aware is essential to good practice in many professions and workplace situations, and is referred to as reflexive practice. But there are sometimes limited opportunities to acquire reflective skills in busy and intensive learning environments where students are expected to take in a lot of information, constantly interact and produce a high volume of output. Although it takes time and commitment, keeping a structured, reflective journal helps to make the learning easier, more direct, more embodied and more personal — by making it your own. When you write about your learning experiences, you claim your own real, personal relationship to the subject matter. Writing a learning journal supports you to practise congruence, self-disclosure and mindful self-aware reflection in relation to the course material. It also provides the opportunity for you to 'catch up' with feelings that are stirred up by the training process. It is important that students are assured of privacy for their writing, and that only selected excerpts from their journals need to be presented, so that they are free of fears relating to assessment, judgment or criticism.

Prompts for reflective learning journals

At the beginning of any training or learning experience, spend time writing down your own learning goals. These may or may not be the same as the defined learning outcomes offered by the program, but write in your own words what is interesting and meaningful to you. Use journalling to help you become a more active learner. Students who are actively engaged in meeting personal goals and who take an active, self-motivated approach to learning report much higher levels of satisfaction than those who wait to 'receive' the input of the course. In fact, for most courses the main benefits you gain are where you have invested yourself the most.

Define, review and refine your learning goals throughout the program.

- What am I gaining from immersing myself in (the topic/approach, etc.), how do I feel about it, and how can I now apply it?

- What has changed for me as a result of this experience/learning/ teaching?

- Where do I feel in flow with this, what brings me into a peak state with this material and where do I lose my engagement?

- Where do I need to focus my attention next to stay on the wave of fresh learning?

- How, when and where can I apply my learning?

- What do I most like about this material?

- Do I have any questions, doubts and areas where I feel unsure, including where I need to seek resources or help?

- Undertake a reading review — what do I want to follow up?

- What have I learned about myself as a learner–practitioner from this experience?

- How can I take this further?

Prompts for advanced learning

Review the learning outcomes or national standards for the training and expertise relevant to your stage of learning and beyond. Identify your strengths and the learning edges where you need further studies, development, practice or resources. Undertake a learning audit of your current level of expertise in this area, and evaluate:

- how far you've come; identify your strengths and achievements

- your unique signature strengths, which include the unique combination of previous learning and life experience that only you can bring

- where you want to get to

- what you need in order to succeed and finish

- what is going well

- what is not going so well and how you can improve on this

- the remaining learning tasks; organize them into categories, and then into windows of time

- significant gaps in your learning that have not been met in the current environment, and envision where and how you can fill these gaps.

WHERE NEXT?

Record and reflect on your hopes and desires for how you want to apply your learning. When you joined the program, some of this was already in your mind. Has it changed? Review your original learning goals, and now that you know what you know, consider your current position and how you want to develop further. What opportunities are now open to you? What new actions can you take to inform people of your new skills, place yourself in the job market, or develop a new project that draws on your enhanced expertise?

JOURNALLING FOR WORK: SELF-MENTORING, COACHING AND SUPERVISION

Mentoring, supervision and coaching can make all the difference — we all have blind spots and there are definitely times when we need an experienced person to support, challenge and nurture us as we grow and get through problems. But your journal is always available. If you maintain your journalling practice through the years, you will demonstrate an enviable degree of self-assurance and clear thinking, and you will have somewhere to go when facing challenges.

HOW TO SET UP A SELF-MENTORING PROGRAM IN YOUR JOURNAL

First of all, establish the qualities, skills, attitudes and knowledge you need in order to be effective at your job. These need to be related to your official job description, as well as the ways in which you relate best to your job as the person that you are. Use the same prompts a good manager, boss, mentor, coach or supervisor would ask you. These will be specific to your situation, but could include:

- target achievement or result

- completion date of the target

- how you feel about your ability to achieve the target

- your hopes and expectations that this will bring to you

- your anxieties, worries and fears. How might these play out? What can you do to keep these in perspective and prevent them from making you delay, procrastinate or get sidetracked?

- a list of resources you'll need

- thinking about how you need to organize your time to ensure success

- considering what you need to put in place to ensure you retain the necessary focus

- listing people to consult during the process and any specific aspects can you ask them for help with

- thinking of ways you might sabotage yourself during this process, and what you can do to address that now so that it does not become a problem down the line

- listing some major obstacles, hindrances or difficulties that you can see coming up; explore these in detail, with the emphasis on how you intend to address each one, if and when needed.

WORKING WITH DIFFICULT OR CHALLENGING COLLEAGUES

Here are some questions to ask yourself if you are working with a person or people you find challenging, to help you gain clarity and provide options for dealing with the situation.

- First of all, determine: is it me or them?

- Who is this person for me? (Think about all the people this person might remind you of. Does this provide any insight as to why you find them annoying or difficult?)

- Why does this person upset/annoy/trigger me so much?

- What can I do to stop reacting to the triggers?

- On reflection, what is the best way for me to handle the situation?

JOURNALLING FOR INDEPENDENT LEARNING AND STUDY

There are many opportunities for independent learning and study available online, and you can enrol in a continuous self-directed professional or personal development program. The same processes for journalling apply when you are studying or learning independently. You can track your learning, progress and development in any area, reflect on your attainment, and clarify your sense of direction and purpose with what you are learning. You can set up appropriate journalling prompts for yourself that support and encourage you to keep on track. In this situation you may find it helpful to create journal templates on a computer, with pre-assigned questions to answer, so that your regular journalling sessions consist of filling these in. For example:

- main learning points

- personal reflections on this material

- how I can apply this to change or improve my work

- action points to follow up.

If you are an active lifelong learner, an important area of reflection is the portfolio of skills, expertise, knowledge and wisdom that you acquire over time and that is completely individual to you. It's possible you may be unique in your combination of specializations. It's worth reflecting in detail on all the possible combinations of your areas of interest and expertise. Many innovations are created by individuals who spill over the edges of predefined subject boundaries and make new combinations that no one else has previously thought of. List your areas of expertise in columns, combine them with each other, and brainstorm what could be created by combining them.

PART 5

Branching out with journalling

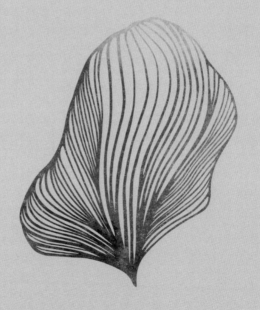

A writer writes, that's all there is to
it. Writing in a journal is no more or
less special than writing a bestseller or
writing for a living. A journal gives you
a space of glorious freedom to explore
anything and everything, and helps you
to stay in the flow.

CHAPTER 11

Journalling for writers

This section does not include everything you need if you are a writer and you journal, but there may be some ideas to take away. Journal writing and being a writer flow into one another, and many great books began in a journal. For anyone who writes, journal writing is a way to practise writing in much the same way as musicians practise scales, exercises and rehearsal pieces — because a writer writes, frequently. They do not hang around waiting for the perfect writing assignment.

Excellent writing may be easy to read and might look like it has been put together very simply, but it takes great skill to write so that readers really want to turn the page or scroll down. A writer can't produce a finished piece of work straight out of his or her head, and writing techniques have to be practised over time. Good quality writing combines clarity and flow. Writing is always difficult even for writers who are good at it, and journal writing can help.

Many writers keep journals, and although the function of the journal may vary, keeping a journal alongside any other daily writing can lubricate the flow. This is just as important for experienced writers as for those just setting out. As any writer knows, being successful as a writer takes a great deal of writing practice, and if you do not have a current writing assignment, as long as you keep a journal you are still writing. A writer writes, usually every day, and the habit of writing is in some ways more important than the topic or content you are writing about.

Brenda Ueland, an acclaimed mid-century novelist and creative writing teacher, wrote in *If You Want to Write* about how her journal helped her as a writer by enabling her to begin to enjoy writing; before keeping a journal she had found writing boring and an immense effort. She learned how to journal to capture the immediacy of her lived experience, thoughts and perceptions.[1] She writes: 'It has shown me that writing is talking, thinking on paper. And the more impulsive and immediate the writing the closer it is to the thinking, which it should be.' This shows the importance of journalling your ideas in progress, the journey you are having, so there is a close observation, attention and engagement with your own process as a writer.

Your journal is the place where you can write down the ideas that come to you when you are busy writing something else. It's the place where you can collect all kinds of ideas, writing prompts and exercises. You can practise writing techniques, explore new directions and ideas, and even journal like a normal person! If you are someone who writes for a living, a journal provides an outlet for free writing where you can follow imaginative or creative impulses without fear of them not meeting the approval of audience or publisher. Journal writing can provide an important release from pressure, where you can explore new directions rather than what you are being paid to write. Having this kind of journal process can make you a better writer, as you can continually expand your repertoire of topics, angles, vocabulary, style, point of view, voice, character and so forth. By allowing yourself regular time for intensive free writing, you allow ideas that are circulating in your subconscious to come into expression. This is a potent form of creative reverie. Who knows how many books and articles began life in a journal, but many great writers keep journals and have always done so. When you are journalling, you are relaxed and in flow, there is no pressure or expectation, you are free of restraint and you are paying close attention to your craft — for the joy of it, or because you must write in order to be you. These are ideal conditions in which creative seeds may emerge and take root.

Regular journal writing will strengthen you as a writer and help you align with the authentic vigour of honest, straightforward self-expression. You will know your own style and voice, you will be in touch with your creativity and inspiration, and develop the fastest possible methods for reaching the flow state, often.

John Steinbeck kept a journal about his process and progress in writing *The Grapes of Wrath*. It's called *Working Days: The journals of the Grapes of Wrath*. It's full of self-doubt, which in a way is encouraging for us all. By the time he was writing this journal his writing was already acclaimed and successful, and yet here we can see him struggling and feeling helpless at times. We can see how his ideas come together, and his working process. He sets his writing goals for the day and discusses his plot development.

Writers also use journalling for practical reasons such as longer-term planning, capturing initial ideas and outlines, working things out, releasing steam, planning and tracking work in progress, submissions tracking, and submissions checklists. This book you are now reading emerged out of a journal writing process, where I was bringing together ideas about how to support students who wanted to engage in productive journal writing. It was a simple working journal to work out these ideas, and this is exactly how books grow from small ideas that are given space to grow and develop on the page. If you believe in an idea, stay with it in your journal, and keep on working with it until it is sufficiently strong and resolved to share.

JOURNAL WRITING TO SUPPORT
THE CREATIVE PROCESS

Creativity researchers have broadly defined four stages of the creative process: preparation, incubation, illumination and verification. First you develop your ideas, engage in research, and then you allow yourself to marinate in the ideas. This second incubation stage may look like you are 'not doing anything'. At a certain point, some of your ideas begin to come together, and you can quite often have a jolt of enthusiasm as you try to get them written down. The verification process involves reviewing and editing the work, in order to fit it for its intended purpose and prepare it to go for publication. Breaking down creativity in this way can make it sound a little dull, but it is helpful to recognize which stage you are in.

THE JOURNAL AS AN OPPORTUNITY
TO HONE YOUR WRITING VOICE

The writing voice can be described as the unique persona from which you write, including the kind of language, sentence structure and attitude that most economically and gracefully expresses your point of view and chosen type of writing. A consistent writing voice is often hard won, easily recognized and inimitable — for example, Hemingway's sparse style influenced generations of writers after him because of its deft authenticity, apparent simplicity and truthfulness. Your writing voice can be related to your speaking voice; it's worth reading your work aloud to yourself to hear how it sounds to the ear. In fact, many writers do 'hear' the words in their head as they write or type them, or imagine how they might sound to an ideal reader. If your speaking voice is completely different from the writing voice or persona you are reaching for, you need to hear the words in your head.

STREAM OF CONSCIOUSNESS WRITING

This type of writing entered the mainstream in many twentieth-century novels, such as in works by Virginia Woolf or James Joyce (and perhaps some people think that this is all that journalling is about, a kind of monologue). At the time, this modernist style was a new development, a way of showing how our relentless internal monologues happen — one thought segues into the next in a blend of conscious and unconscious, and this was a kind of investigation into consciousness. Techniques for capturing the flow of consciousness are still a valid form of enquiry into your own thought processes — using any method you can to write down everything that comes to mind without censoring it, so that you can see for yourself the kind of thought processes and material that are constantly flowing through your mind.

We think literally thousands of thoughts every day, and you cannot possibly capture them all, but you can try a technique similar to that of a moth collector who captures a sample of moths in a location by shining a light onto a white sheet in the night, to catch whichever moths come. To try this, ensure you are deeply relaxed and comfortable, and will not be distracted. You need to be in a peaceful, unfocused state of reverie, and allow your mind to soften and let go. You want to enter a state of mind similar to when you begin the process of falling asleep. Images and words will stream through your mind, and you need to stay awake enough that you can write some of these down, yet deeply relaxed enough that you don't analyze or censor them, or get caught up in them. You are not the editor at this time, any more than the moth collector can choose which moths will arrive on a certain night. Do this a few times, then go back as an editor and have a look at what you have captured.

DEEPEN AND EXTEND YOUR LINGUISTIC INTELLIGENCE

Any and all writers can benefit from journal exercises where you push past imitations and boundaries, develop your capacity for written expression, and go out beyond your comfort zone into something new, where you may perhaps surprise yourself. American psychologist Howard Gardner explored how poets, in particular, demonstrate high linguistic intelligence in the way they use language. In his book *Frames of Mind: The theory of multiple intelligences*, he goes into detail about how poets exploit underlying features of language and are aware of much more than the meaning of words, including word order, sounds, rhythms, rhyme, how words look on the page, inflection and metre. Poets use this multisensitivity more extensively than other writers, in that in poetry (as in music) the method by which something is conveyed is at least as important as the content or meaning.

All writers can benefit from the kinds of warm-up exercises that poets regularly engage in. These include, for example, making yourself write something in a restrictive form, such as a sonnet, a villanelle, a 100-word story or a 200-word blog post. By making yourself work hard to fit something decent into the rules of the form, you have to be original, creative and resourceful. This produces creative tension, but also offers you a certain support and freedom at the same time. The exercise works well once you get through your resistance to the arbitrary restriction of the form, and you might be amazed at the quality of your piece! Another technique poets use is to work with poems by other writers and cannibalize them in various ways, such as 'writing back' to the narrator, or responding to them with another poem, making your own 'version' of the poem or 'translating' poems written in a language you do not speak, or only vaguely understand, and making your own poem based on what you think the original poem is about, or what you would like it to be about. You can respond to other works of art such as paintings, songs or a symphony: immerse yourself wholeheartedly in the work, and write down all that comes. A technique used by poets working in the surrealist tradition is to gather found text from different sources and combine different pieces. This is the basis writing a good poem using just poetry fridge magnets! Bringing together materials that are incongruous, completely unexpected, out of context or disparate can stimulate fresh work.

A few writing prompts for writers

One writing idea leads to another, and what can begin as a way of trying to work something out, record a conversation, express your frustration or take notes can lead to a new idea that simply opens up in front of you. The more time you spend in the zone where you are writing in flow, whatever the topic, the more this happens. Use your journal to capture a conversation overheard on the bus, write down writing advice that inspires you, collect phrases and sentences, or capture random ideas that arise. Use your journal to capture your acute observations of your daily life and bring the attitude of a traveller to writing about your experience.

Write 'letters' or write from imagined parts of yourself

Many writers have engaged in an exchange of letters about their work and these are sometimes drafted in the journal first, or a copy is kept in the journal. Using this process, you can write letters to and from anyone, whether you send them or not.

Give written advice to your present self from an imagined more experienced or more confident version of yourself, who can give you wise counsel as a writer. Write to yourself now as the much more experienced writer you will become in the future. This voice must be positive and benevolent and not harsh. You can also practise writing to yourself in the imagined voice of another writer, perhaps a well-known one, who can help you identify your own voice more clearly.

The bookshelf prompt

Take your journal to a library or a well-stocked bookshelf in your home or, preferably, that of a friend. Half close your eyes and read the titles of the books as they come to you. Write down the titles, as you perceive them. Then write the first paragraphs for these titles, as you imagine them, as books you might be intrigued to read or write.

Lists for writers

Many poems are based on lists, and you can see lists inside them. Once your list is flowing, you will find places within it you can develop further. Here are a few randomly generated prompts for lists, and you can easily craft your own.

- Collect words.

- Gather observations.

- List the reasons why you love and hate the colour blue.

- List your favourite patterned fabrics and where they can be found.

- Write down twenty reasons why you should never give up.

- Give advice to someone about things to do when they are bored.

- List all the dragons, unicorns or other mythical or magical beings you have seen in your life and what they could have been telling you.

- List the titles of a series of paintings in a gallery.

- Write down ten things you thought you'd forgotten.

- List all the things a whale sees.

- Write out the laws of a new world, planet or society.

- List all the dreams you can remember.

- List ten very tiny things and ten enormous things and what connects them.

- Raid reference sources, for example on subjects such as astronomy, taxonomy or lepidoptery, copy out lists of this data and intersect it with other found texts or lines of your own text on completely different subjects or in a completely different style.

- Write lists directly connected to your writing practice, such as lists of writing tips, things to remember, words, writers you admire, and all the writing project ides that come to you, so that they are available when you need them.

NOTES

....

....

....

....

....

....

....

....

....

....

....

....

JOURNAL WRITING FOR READERS

Do you enjoy reading but find that a few months later you have forgotten most of what you read? Would you like to go back to favourite books and just read a few selected highlights or a reminder of the main points that you took from the book? Or do you need to read for a course of study but have difficulty organizing and retaining useful information? Set up a 'Books I Have Read' journal — but not one that is lame and pointless like some of the pre-printed ones.

A good writer is also a good reader, and the ability to respond to what you are reading helps your reading become an active engagement rather than a passive activity. This is one reason why book groups are popular. Books are written as part of an ongoing dialogue among a community of readers and writers. Join them in articulating your own thoughts on the page. Even if, for now, your thoughts stay within your journal, this is much more empowering than reading in a passive way. There's no fear of judgment while you begin to shape your own thinking. By giving yourself permission to talk back to the author, your own ideas become more formed and grounded, and you will be able to make more active use of these ideas in the months to come, without even thinking about it. Here are a few suggestions.

- If this is going to be useful, you may need to allow a different amount of space, and even different headings, for each book. For this reason, set up your own blank journal rather than buy a pre-printed book journal. Try completing two to three entries on a scratch pad first, so that you develop the structure that is going to work best for you. This book can last you a long time and can become a really useful reference source. Headings you might consider would be: title, author, date of publication, date you completed reading, summary of important points/what you got from reading this book/applications (how you can directly benefit from this book by applying it in specific situations), new skills or understanding.

- If you need to refer back to your reading for your own writing, you can adapt a version of the Cornell note-taking system (see page 154).

- List the book title, topic and date. Include all the publication details you will need for future referencing so you never have to hunt around for them.

- Key points and main topics (just the ones that are relevant to you!). Under this heading include your notes, formulated in your own words, of what you perceive to be the key points related to the main topics, from your point of view and for your own purpose, so you never have to read through the book again to find this.

- Essential quotations. If there are some fantastic phrases written by the author, then copy a few, or if there are more than a few you could highlight them in the actual book or mark the pages with sticky notes, and list the page numbers here with a brief indication of what each quote is about.

- Summary. Under this heading, summarize succinctly the essence of your notes, in your own words.

A journal habit is a resource for life and a wonderful doorway to hold open for any young person. Playing in a journal brings multisensory benefits to help children discover self-directed focus, imagination and self-awareness without using a screen or device.

CHAPTER 12

Journalling with children

Sometimes a new journal is a wonderful gift for a child. Most of the approaches in this book are intended for adults, but journal writing is a great resource for children, teenagers and young people. If you are keeping a journal, you could suggest your children keep one too, and if they see you enjoy journalling they may want to join in. You could create a family journal together or buy them a special journal of their own and help them set it up. Depending on the child and their age, they may need structure and guidance and some children could feel at a loss with a blank book, whereas others will want to do it their own way. You might need to help them establish subject headings and writing prompts — or purchase a pre-printed journal with prompts suitable to their age and interests. The *Ally's World* series by Karen McCombie is based upon fictional journals, and *My V. Groovy Journal (Ally's World)* is a journal with lots of prompts that children enjoy.

You will need to support the young person to provide sufficient guidance, inspiration, ideas and resources, but without being in any way controlling or intrusive or wanting their journal to turn out a certain way. Some children will really enjoy journalling and will not want much direction, and will want to steer their own creative output, while others will be uninterested. It is essential that the young person knows this is a private space for them and you will not be reading it without their permission. If they find out you have read it without asking, or if you criticize anything they have written, this is a betrayal of trust that is likely to affect your relationship permanently. They may also need help to ensure it is stored out of reach of other family members, and that they have private space for journal writing.

Journalling is a significant resource for children and young people who are having a difficult time, for any reason. The benefits of journalling — such as increased health, wellbeing, confidence, self-esteem and self-authorship — apply just as much to young people as to adults. Starting a journal habit when you are young sets you up with a fantastic resource for life, to help you cope, to work things out and to have a place to go with difficult and confusing feelings that no one else understands. One of the best things you can do is give a child a nice journal (or even a trashy one such as a *Wreck This Journal* book) and — only if they ask — some ideas for how to have fun with it. You could say something about how journalling helped you through difficult times. It has to be clear that this has nothing to do with writing for school, it is just for them, it will never be judged, and that they can do whatever they want with it, you won't read it and you won't overreact about anything they write if they do show it to you.

Writing prompts for young children

This is the easiest age group to engage in a journal writing habit, though they may want to scribble all over your journal too! They will appreciate encouragement, praise and suggestions.

- A creative journal: writing stories, poems, drawings around a theme.

- An enriched diary record of a time of change and transition can help children process and come to terms with changes in their lives.

- Writing about a trip or an activity, family life or pets, perhaps in scrapbook format with photos, collage and art.

- What are your favourite magical superpowers? How would you like to use them to change the world?

Writing prompts for middle years children

Keeping your own diary record of your personal experience, from your own point of view and perspective is an important beginning in being able to establish a personal sense of self.

- Write an 'About Me' page.

- Write lists of your favourite things, perhaps with collage elements.

- Use it as a space to explore how you feel and think about challenging events.

- Write about memories from when you were younger.

- What do you think your life will be like in ten or twenty years?

- What advice would you like to give your teachers and parents?

- What would you like your adult self to know and understand about your childhood?

- If you had to describe your world to a visiting alien, what are the things you would like to explain to them?

- Write (imaginary) letters to famous people.

- Set up a correspondence diary — your child or teen engages in a correspondence with you. You take it in turns to write something, then the other person affirms and responds. It can be a good way to discuss topics that might be difficult to speak about, and the timing of the entries and responses is determined by the young person; you respond to him or her when you receive a message in the journal. You can leave it on each other's pillow or an agreed personal space.

Writing prompts for teenagers and young people

The search for one's own sense of self is much more insistent from adolescence onwards, and there's a need for private space to work things out. A journal can be a great ally as long as it really is private, as teenagers need space to explore and experiment with thoughts and ideas they are probably not going to follow through on. Pre-written prompts for teenagers may hit the right note, and they can easily find their own on social media.

- Write about what you value about your friends; what do you look for in a friend?

- Write about what makes you interesting and unique, and where you fit in with your peers.

- What are the important things you wish you could say to parents, teachers, peers and anyone, that they wouldn't listen to?

- Write about the ways in which you feel both the same as and different from your family.

- Write letters to family members, famous people or anyone you would like to know how you feel. You don't ever have to show it to them, but you could write a version for them later if you decide you would like them to receive it.

- Make a scrapbook or collage with photos of friends, and include a quote or a typical comment from each one.

- What is special about your peer group at school or college, your friends and the way you do things? Are there things the adults do not get?

- Write about songs you love, or write your own song lyrics.

- Make a colour journal. Creating a colour art journal is an apparently simple and easy approach to journalling, where you devote an art journal, or one section of it, to each colour. The person creating the journal chooses colours based on what colours look brightest and most attractive to them. Images in the chosen colours can be assembled and blended — for example if the colour is turquoise, turquoise seas and Caribbean beaches can be blended with fashion photos, art, graffiti and creative writing. The colour turquoise is associated with the qualities of the thymus chakra — cleansing and refreshing — and the young person can write about how turquoise makes them feel. This is not demanding or confronting, but it can be surprisingly enjoyable and enriching. Everyone can have their own personal relationship to a colour, and will find special, surprising, personal connections to the colour.

A journal can be a great ally as long as it really is private, as teenagers need space to explore and experiment with thoughts and ideas they are probably not going to follow through on.

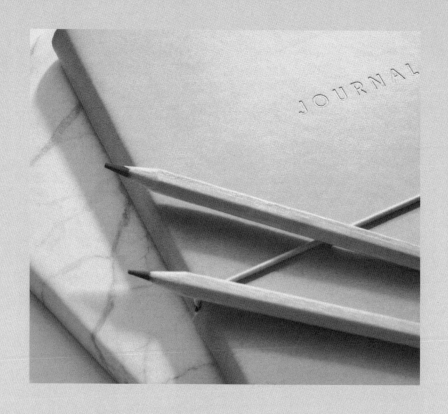

Try something new and see where it takes you. Bring variety into your journalling practice to keep it fresh and exciting.

CHAPTER 13

Further types of journalling

There are no limits to the ways in which you can enjoy journalling. Here are a few further suggestions for you to try. You can create a unique combination of different approaches that is flexible in response to your changing needs.

LIST CURATION

As a journaller you can curate some special, creative and unusual lists. You probably already keep lists, such as to-do lists, shopping lists or lists of ingredients for a recipe, but there are many more exciting lists you can try. Many of these are ideal for the bullet journal format (as a collection) or you can make a dedicated book for your list collection. Lists are a fun way to capture the essence of anything — the ten best places to visit in Spain, your twenty favourite fragrances, 25 reasons to be happy, the best parties you can remember. Lists are a means of capturing anything and everything in a meaningful format. List-making can enlarge the scope of your journalling, because lists can include things to do, things to remember, visions, dreams and goals, checklists, ideas to try, memories you don't want to lose, inventories, lists of materials and processes. If a new idea comes to you, add it to an ideas list. Regular list-writing can help you keep your journalling upbeat; for example, you can begin a normal journalling session with a list of 'the ten most important things to focus on today'.

Here are a few ideas to get you started on lists in your journal.

POP-UP LISTS

The pop-up list is the best invention ever. You probably have them in lots of different locations — across your desk top, fridge or diary. The sticky note is a core tool, and it can become part of your journal life — keep sticky notes in your journal. You can make a distinction between curated lists, which have their own designated journal space, and pop-up lists which can come to you at any time, and that you are likely to visit while you are journalling about something else. Keep a space for pop-up lists on your pages or keep sticky notes handy. You will be in good company, as many brilliant thinkers capture random lists of ideas while they are focusing on their work. Once you move into the flow state while you are journalling, you never know what type of ideas will emerge and this is part of what makes journalling such an exciting journey.

THE PERMANENT CHECKLIST

There's also the permanent checklist that can save you time and anxiety. Rather than starting from scratch each time you need a list, you simply have permanent lists that you can refer to time and time again. These can include a packing list for each type of trip, a school uniform or sports kit list, financial record items to send to your accountant, supplies or groceries to keep in stock, your car registration details, the clothing and shoe sizes of anyone you buy for, or any information you need from time to time and have to hunt for. Think how much nicer it will feel to have all this information neatly labelled in one book that you keep in a special secret place!

POP-UP LISTS EXAMPLE

Reminders to maintain my space and keep it feeling ordered and peaceful:

- Declutter and take out the old toys and clothes this month.

- Fresh colours this year — maybe spring green and white with pink or teal.

- Make my own aromatherapy mist, remember to spray!

- Re-organize book shelves, maybe arrange books by colour not topic.

- New area rug for living room?

Lists for journallers

- Secret goals you want to achieve this year

- My ongoing work projects

- Five- or ten-year goals

- Career goals

- Personal dreams and goals

- A daily gratitude or celebration list

- Things that made me happy today

- All the things I did today

- My intentions for this month

- My achievements this month/last month

- My personal strengths

- The things I'm progressing on

- Compliments and positive feedback I have received

- My greatest accomplishments

- Twenty reasons why I am awesome

- All the things I love about him or her

- The things I know and understand more than anyone else

- Complete the list 'It's time to ...'

- Complete the list 'What I truly want and desire is ...'

- Complete the list 'From today, I ...'

- The goals, intentions and wishes that never make it onto my working to-do lists

- Things to do when I have unexpected free time

- Things to do in my local area, and staycation ideas

- Places to visit

- My weekly routine

- Fitness tracker

- People to contact

- Books, movies, videos, podcasts or music that I love

- Music, movies or books I want read, watch or listen to

- Playlists to make

- Websites, blogs, online journals and other sources

- Favourite memories with [ ]ld

- Favourite memories from c[ ]od

- Favourite memories with my partner

- An inventory of books enjoyed
- An inventory of my journals
- Ideas and light bulb moments that come to you
- Processes you want to try (e.g. techniques, tips and hacks, instructions)
- A rolling to-do list, so that what is not completed is moved onto the next list (as in a bullet journal)
- A checklist of life areas and tasks to keep up with and attend to over a three- to twelve-month period
- An annual checklist

- Reminders (e.g. appointments, celebrations, milestones, firsts, anniversaries, birthdays, passwords, pet vaccinations and treatments, medication, bills)
- Things that need fixing
- Not-to-do list
- Bucket lists of things you want to try or do, such as trips to plan
- Recipes and ingredients to try
- Shopping lists
- A sleep tracker
- Inspiring quotes
- New words
- New ideas to explore
- Ideas for outfits and fashion combinations
- Nail polish or home décor colours (each colour with a painted-in sample)
- Places to visit

A RECORD-KEEPING OR OBSERVATIONAL JOURNAL

A record-keeping journal is the simplest idea: you record important events, data, feelings and situations that you would like to log or remember, on an ongoing regular basis, as soon as you can after they have happened. The journal is all about your fresh, in-the-moment experience of what has just taken place or that you have witnessed or observed. An observational journal can include visual elements such as sketches or photos. You can make an observational journal about dates, dreams, activities or hobbies, trips, conversations, events, anniversaries, the journey to reach significant goals, or the process of working towards milestones. You could observe the wildlife in your local park over a season, record your observations of your child growing up, write about the customers in your local café over a year, or tell a story about events and life unfolding in your neighbourhood. It is a story that combines time, place, characters and themes, but the story generally unfolds with the passing of time. Some observational journals have evolved into published books because the fresh, vivid, immediate description of local life and place can be compelling. You can also write this form of journal as a blog. If you intend to publish your work and write about living people who could be identified, it is advisable to fictionalize your characters to avoid any potential problems.

YOUR BLOG AS A JOURNAL

A blog is a popular method of self-expression where the writer engages with a subject with passion and enthusiasm. The blogging format is often wordy and loops around its subject in an informal or chatty way. It is often a form of reflective writing. Through exploring and sharing research and ideas, the writer comes to new conclusions. A blog post often ends on an upbeat note, in order to lead the reader to the next instalment.

You can blog about any subject, whether it is taking the rubbish out, your experience of taking the children to school, testing out products or recipes, being a gay single parent, your studies in astronomy and astrophysics, the rise and fall of a job or relationship, or your book and film reviews. You probably have your favourite blogs, but have you considered writing your own? For readers it can be fascinating to get close to another person's personal preoccupations and find out all kinds of details about how they live and think. It is like hearing from a friend. For you as a writer there are many benefits. In the process of writing a blog over time, you can establish your unique authorial point of view. You can find original ways to connect with your subject matter and your readers. One advantage of a blog journal is that you are writing for an audience, and practising relating to your readers. Their comments can inform and inspire further posts or ideas for articles or publications (although you will need to immunize yourself against spam and trolls). There are no editorial restrictions if you are the owner of your own website where you post. Successful blog writers with thousands of followers started out by writing about what was really calling their attention, and learned from feedback about how to make this valuable and relevant to their audience.

Blog posts can vary in length from 200 to 750 words to 2000 words. A blog post needs to be accessible and readable, with images you can access from stock websites (be sure to check they are free and available for you to use). People reading online are less tolerant of reading long paragraphs of text as it takes longer and is more difficult than reading a book or a magazine, and so they are likely to skim over anything that looks too wordy. Your writing must be easy to read, and the reader needs to be given strong motivation for reading, in that the post promises a benefit or a way of understanding or solving a problem that your readers will recognize. This is why blog posts are often given punchy titles and headings. 'Ten ways to ensure your new date finds you completely fascinating' is more likely to be read and enjoyed than 'A blow by blow account of my first date and everything that I talked about'. You are writing about the same material that you might write in your journal about your dating experiences, but the emphasis is different because you are equally considering the needs of the reader alongside your own need for self-expression.

The other important thing about blogging is that you need to provide consistent output. Writing the occasional article when you feel like it will not bring you any followers. You need to provide your readers with a drip feed of regular material. Many blog writers create a lot of material, and then divide it up to be spoon fed to the audience in small pieces. There is software available that enables you to publish blog posts according to pre-assigned schedules.

You can create a video blog or a podcast rather than a written blog, but you still need to prepare the script that you deliver.

TRAVEL JOURNALLING

Travel journalling is fun and helps you get even more from your trip, as you get to create and enjoy a lovely travel journal as a keepsake. You can take a scrapbook style or art journal approach, by collaging in tickets, boarding passes, photos, maps and items such as local flyers, with comments, captions and short descriptive pieces of text. You can take a diary approach and write as you go, adding frequent short entries that capture the immediate experience. Or you can take a more literary approach and step back and write about your experiences and observations in a reflective or more analytical style, once you are home and back at your desk. If you enjoy reading travel books, and you enjoy travelling, try writing your own travel articles or travel blog from your own unique point of view. Your unique perceptions of the places you visit are what makes your writing special. As you gather together a body of work your special travel themes will become clear, and the special benefits you experience from travel.

NEW INSPIRATION FOR LIFELONG JOURNALLERS

If you have been journalling for years and you already know what journalling can do for you, it can help to take a fresh approach from time to time. It's possible you may have planted yourself firmly in one particular approach to journalling, and it may benefit you take a step back and review your process and your practice. Are you getting all you want and need from your journal writing? Could you try some new approaches? Do you journal just in one way? Are your journals either too disorganized or too controlled or too similar? Could you expand your repertoire? How satisfied are you with your journalling practice, and how do you think it could be improved? Do you need to make it more interesting, exciting or inspiring? Or do you want to try extending your journalling practice for some specific focus and results? Hopefully this book can remind you of what a great resource your journalling can be, and you can renew your commitment and expand your repertoire.

You could begin by collecting together your old journals and going through them. When you look back over them, how does it make you feel? If these are positive feelings, how can you intensify the benefits of this in your current journal practice? If these are less than positive feelings, did the journal writing accomplish its purpose at the time? What can you learn for future journalling? Best of all, are there some brilliant ideas or aspects of yourself hidden in your journals that you have not yet developed?

Prompts for experienced journallers to deepen and enrich your journal practice

- Listen carefully to what is calling you to write. Allow yourself to listen and follow the soft, subtle nudges that are beckoning you in a new and as-yet unknown direction. Remember that whatever you want to explore or do, journalling alongside can help you do it better.

- Listen to your body. Have a dialogue with your body and let it have a voice in your journal. John Lee, author of *Writing From the Body: For writers, artists, and dreamers who long to free their voice*, works with a process called 'writing from the body'. Ask your body questions, such as what messages it has for you, and what it knows. Consider that your body is never wrong and has a perspective that can be invaluable to you, as it knows everything about you, and knows important information that you do not know.

- Write for connection. Write a conversation with anyone, or anything, on any aspect of yourself that you would like to know better. Through writing you can realize more of what you know, and discover that you know more than you thought you knew!

- Try new journalling techniques that you may not have considered before as a way of accessing new and unfamiliar aspects of yourself. For example, create an art journal on a specific theme, a gratitude and celebration journal, or a bullet journal, or bring in some self-coaching or mindfulness aspects.

- Focus on a success orientation in your journals. Rather than diarizing your life, move this process forward and write directly for success. Believe in yourself in your journals, and write from your innermost self.

- Create a learning journal as a means to learn something new or train yourself in a new process, without the need to pay for tuition or mentoring.

- Create a workbook journal around a topic that you know quite lot about. Then consider how you might be able to share this with others, for example as an e-book. If you have already been journalling for a number of years then you will have something special you can share with others, albeit in an edited form. This can be a naturally enjoyable process to share with others some of the benefits and discoveries of your journalling practice.

- Write all that you know, that you may have never told anyone, all in one place.

- Make a journalling treat for yourself by creating a beautifully laid out and inspiring journal book, perhaps with prompts that you design for yourself. Now that you have read this handbook, you can put to bed any ideas about your journalling being unimportant, insignificant or 'just about me' or something that you squeeze into a few precious minutes. Make a more central, respectful place in your life for your journal play and recreation. Journalling is being present with yourself, and is always fresh, current and regenerative. You can develop your own unique journalling approach and maybe other people can benefit from this too? There is nothing more powerful than a person who is able to be fully present with themselves and grounded in who they are, and who is then able to help others. Journal writing trains you in the habits of being authentic, truthful, real and present to what is. It helps you to stand in your own place, stop comparing yourself with others, become more inner directed (in a good way) and be the real you that only you can be.

- Use journalling to deepen your reflective practice in your work, if this is relevant to the kind of work you do. This might mean extending your journalling practice and experience to other areas of life, and coming out as a journaller.

- Set up a journalling group — like a book group, but a group where you discuss journal writing, compare experiences, share tips and inspiration, spend time writing together and read famous journals and books about journalling. Spending time writing in your journal with others is surprisingly enjoyable and uplifting.

Your journal is a place
in the centre of your own circle,
a container for
the alchemy of your life.

SHAMANISTIC JOURNALLING: NEW JOURNALLING IDEAS

You don't need to train as shaman to feel your own connection to the millennia-old wisdom traditions of the Indigenous peoples across the world. You can directly connect to these traditions — they belong to you, as we are all descended from various combinations of Indigenous peoples. This is not disrespectful to specific living traditions that hold their own perspectives, as shamanism is very much about being aware of the perspective that we each hold. One way you can do this is to draw on shamanic principles in your journalling. In western psychology, there are said to be two main areas of life that we are preoccupied with — work and money, relationships and pleasure — that require our full-hearted engagement if we are to attain fulfilment. Shamanistic perspectives have always held two more: connection to earth and nature, and connection to spirit, the unseen, oneness, source or glue that holds all the worlds together. As humans, we are the bridge between all the worlds of the seen and the unseen, material and spiritual, manmade and natural. We integrate all of these in the living process of our lives. A further important aspect of shamanic traditions is the honouring of the ancestors, and feeling that you are part of the flow of life from the past into the present, and beyond — sometimes depicted as a river of living blood. Although these traditions have been seen as diametrically opposed to modern science, religion and rationalism, and therefore primitive or unimportant, their resurging popularity indicates they fill a need that is not met by science, religion, commerce or family life alone, and that many people are seeking a richer, more enhanced texture to their sense of identity and belonging to the world. We seek to interact with the natural world in meaningful ways that go beyond merely consuming it or observing it. So how can we apply this to some journal practices?

All shamanistic and magical ceremonies begin with a circle. The medicine wheel and the witch's circle are a fundamental language of wholeness. The medicine wheel is a circle that represents all the geographical directions, and each direction is also associated with certain qualities, for example:

A MEDICINE WHEEL

N
WINTER

ancestors, earth, black, midnight, maturity, caves, mountains, rocks and crystals, strength, the body, the place of darkness

W
AUTUMN

water, death, old age, dreams, feelings, compassion, intuition, lakes, rivers and oceans, the place of the setting sun

THE CENTRE WHERE YOU ARE FROM

the place of balanced perspective, interdependence, connection to all beings

E
SPRING

wisdom, teachings, air, wind, breath, intellect, music, light, dawn, high places, clouds, the place of the rising sun

S
SUMMER

fire, emotions, red, courage, willpower, passion, energy, sun, stars, lightning, heat, volcanoes, deserts, the place of light

There are many different variations in different traditions, so there is not a universal agreement on the individual meaning of the different positions. However, there is a universal agreement on the value of the different positions — that they are of equal value, and each position occupies its own place on the great wheel of life. Each position exists in relationship to every other position, and there are also correspondences and connections across the wheel, for example the cycles of the seasons, growth and decay, seed and fruit.

Your journal is a place in the centre of your own circle, a container for the alchemy of your life. Shamans perceive that whatever we want to achieve, create or eliminate from our lives, we have to be aligned with a clear intention that is grounded by knowing who we are and where we stand on the wheel of our life. This is linked with the idea of 'writing in the round' that was discussed on page 69. Each one of us has a unique position where we have something special to say. Everyone is implicitly interconnected on the great wheel of life, and the wheel itself is eternal while the individual forms that inhabit it are temporary. At the centre of the wheel is a great space, the void, that represents the great spirit, source, oneness and interconnectivity.

In addition to holding a model or vision of the wholeness and interconnection of all life, and that the unseen is the energy that drives the seen, many shamanic traditions place great emphasis on vision and intent — qualities that are understood to be necessary to underlie effective action in the world. Although a modern person might consider it absurd, a shaman would never undertake any important action without consultation, agreement and harmony between the different forces involved in this action and which are likely to be affected by it. She or he would not open a mine to take rocks and crystals without consultation with the earth beings or the people who live in the village near the mine, or leave the ground in a complete mess afterwards. Rock and crystals, and the underground realm, are understood to have their own consciousness, and if they are not consulted and informed about the mining process they might be unhappy about it and this might have a negative effect upon the village, and so forth. We may think that this worldview is quaint, anthropomorphic, naïve or ignorant, because if we hold assumptions that other life forms are not sentient and are only commodities for our use, we have no connection with them, and we can take and use them however we want without thought of any consequences.

The quality of informed action, action supported by the base of a holistic worldview and an understanding that all actions have consequences on other beings, including those we cannot see, is described in the shamanistic terms vision and intent. This sense of purpose and informed action requires an understanding of where the practitioner is standing on the circle, and who and what he or she desires to change or influence. To enable this informed understanding, a shamanic practitioner holds the quality of unconditional love towards all the parties involved.

This brief explanation may be sufficient to introduce ideas of shamanic-inspired journal writing. In shamanistic work, as in journalling, intent underlies everything. It is a central concept that underlines the complexity of shamanistic theory and thought. Your intention when committing to taking an action is everything. Your intention is what has the furthest reaching and most transformative results, rather than the facts of going through the motions of performing tasks. Within the shamanistic worldview, setting your intention is the way that you bridge the seen and unseen realities, as you need to work with both the seen and unseen worlds in order to make something happen — inner and outer, above and below, manifest and potential, spirit and matter. In a shamanic approach you know that the spirit or unseen aspects of reality are working alongside you, and this knowledge and trust frees you up. When you set a clear and deliberate intention, you as a human being are balanced between all of these forces, and this makes you powerful and creative.

SHAMANISTIC JOURNALLING PROMPTS

A selection of new journalling ideas to engage your imagination and creativity and to help you be playful.

The power animal

A power animal is an animal spirit that agrees to be your ally. You allow your power animal to come to you, rather than go hunting for it, for example in a dream or during a ceremony designed for the purpose of relaxing your conscious mind, or any method you like for allowing the image or sense of a wild creature to come to you. You probably already have your favourite animals and birds. Write imagined meetings and dialogues with them; you could ask them for guidance, for example. In a shamanic approach, imagination is a viable way to access information from your timeless sense of self rather than your logical mind.

Becoming the other

Focus your attention on an animal, plant, person, a rock, a tree, or anything. While you focus your attention on it, half close your eyes and breathe to synchronize your breath with it. Allow yourself to imagine you are the rock or the cat. Feel as they feel. Write from this 'I am' perspective. This is an ancient way of obtaining knowledge — it's not about the thing in an objective scientific way, but from within the experience of loosening your self-identification and re-patterning your awareness to align with something or someone other than your small self. Your words will become more cat-like or rock-like. Choose an object you want a close association with or want to learn from, such as tree for learning about patience and peacefulness.

Dialogue with other sentient beings

Go to any plant or tree with your notebook. Request an audience, have a conversation, ask questions, find out about life from this different perspective. You might feel a little self-conscious having a chat with a tree but if you really get involved in the process, this will be much more interesting than worrying about what passing strangers think about you. Ignore any ideas about how crazy this is and enter into the spirit of it.

Listen

Listen to anyone or anything. Simply listen without judgment, and then write down what you hear. Listen with your inner ear, not just to any words that are spoken.

A GOAL MANIFESTATION PROCESS

Will is the process of creating and expressing coherence by residing in the centre of your circle, and not being locked out into a place on the periphery where you are less informed, less whole and out of balance. Creating something that you want involves applying all of yourself to your goals, and then at the same time being able to get out of your own way in order to nourish the new possibilities into being. First of all, defining your goals takes time and quality attention, and your journal is the place to write all of this down. Here is a shamanistic-style exercise to help you practise working with the energetic aspects of setting a goal into motion. You need to practise this exercise until it becomes easy and relaxed. It needs to become something you are familiar with that does not feel like much of an effort.

Breathe, relax, ground yourself and become centred. Relax into your sense of being here now, as you, within your own sense of presence. Rest your attention in your breath, and just observe your breathing while you stay present in your centre. You may like to imagine your centre is in your heart area. Your sense of purpose originates here, not in your head. See if you can locate your sense of purpose, and then tune in to it, rest your attention in it and feel it. Allow yourself time to enjoy how it feels, the qualities you experience. You might observe a rising sense of energy, it might be strong or faint but with a distinct tone that may already be familiar to you from times when, for example, you feel excited and decide to do something you really want to do.

Now allow this feeling of uprising energy to radiate into the environment around you. Observe how it feels to let this energy flow outwards. Now, allow this energy to connect with a goal. For the practice exercise, envisage a goal that you know you can achieve within a week or two; keep it simple, because you just want to have the experience before you apply it to something really important. Decide on something that you would like to do or achieve or bring about. Imagine the energy of your sense of purpose infusing your goal and both of them radiating into the world together. It helps if you are not too emotionally attached to whether you achieve the goal, and don't choose something you are anxious about. Say the goal aloud to yourself and write it down, so it is clear what you are focusing on. Carry on with your life, but be sure to engage in continuing actions that will help in progressing towards your goal, for however long it takes.

So here is the process:

- Define your aim or goal and write it down; get it really clear and write a statement about it: I want to ... I am going to ... I intend to ...

- Become present and relaxed.

- Locate and tune in to your sense of purpose, and pay attention to how it feels.

- Allow this energy to rise and radiate into your surroundings.

- Now allow your goal to connect with this energy as it radiates outwards into the world and into any places connected with the desired outcome.

- Engage in activities that help bring about your goal, including any ideas or opportunities that you become aware of.

In order to shut the door firmly on the old and welcome in the new, you need to be fully aware of all that you are letting go of. It's not enough to decide to change and let something go. Even if you end the relationship or leave the job, the patterning that enabled you to set it up in the first place will persist until you can be really clear and specific about what it is and how you were vulnerable to this happening.

A PROSPERITY JOURNAL

A journal is the ideal space in which to set up, organize and follow through on processes to increase your level of prosperity. Prosperity thinking or prosperity consciousness is not directly about wealth creation, although it can help you get there. It's about identifying with a positive mindset where you enjoy and appreciate all that you already have. The first stage of working towards creating prosperity consciousness is to stop believing in your limitations and instead focus on what you love doing and are passionate about, what you are really interested in. The desire to acquire wealth is not motivating enough on its own. Through loving what you do, you can create opportunities to increase your potential. There is a link between self-worth and financial worth in that you need to believe in yourself and what you do, and in what you are capable of. This self-belief is the hallmark of anyone who has achieved financial success or independence.

A LUNAR JOURNAL

Some people like to organize their schedules by the lunar rather than the calendar month. By working in sync with the moon cycles, you can make use of the way that the moon may be affecting you at different times, and enjoy the feeling that you are working in harmony with nature. The only way to see if this works for you is to try it with a project that you start to envisage and plan around the time of the dark moon and new moon, and begin to put into action during the early phases of the waxing moon. From a shamanic perspective, timing is always an important factor in the success of a project, and timing is often measured according to natural cycles, as the Gregorian calendar is man-made. You do not need to purchase a special moon journal, but look up the phases of the moon online and add this information to your journal or diary. The different phases of the moon are linked with different phases in the creative cycle, as described below. Over the course of a few months, note down which phases of the lunar cycle feel most productive for you in different ways, for example when you feel like journalling and reflecting, when you feel like getting things done, when you feel like sharing and getting involved with others, and when you feel like decluttering, organizing and cleaning up. Here is the received wisdom on the ways to use the different moon phases. The emphasis is on beginning during the early moon phases, and reviewing or wrapping up a project in the later phases.

The two to three days of the dark moon are an ideal time for planning and journalling. The new moon is the time for coming up with new ideas. Even if you don't know where something may lead, and you're in the dark, it's a time to sow new seeds in your journal and set up new ideas, intentions, journals and projects. What are you beginning? What will it feel like when you have achieved your desired outcome? Follow any impulses or nudges to try things out by journalling them.

The next phases of the moon are as follows:

- **WAXING CRESCENT MOON.** Move from planning into action, and begin to take active steps towards making your project happen. Tidy up, and put everything in place.

- **THE FIRST QUARTER MOON** occurs one week after the new moon and is the time to begin gathering momentum. Identify actions to take and to follow through on.

- **WAXING GIBBOUS MOON.** At this time, reflect on how you can refine and improve your goal, while continuing to follow through.

- During the **FULL MOON**, reflect upon and celebrate what you have attained during this cycle. Compared with how things were when you set out at new moon, how does it look now?

- **A WANING GIBBOUS MOON** offers the time to disseminate and share your project.

- **LAST QUARTER MOON.** Let go and release anything that does not serve you or that you no longer need.

- **WANING CRESCENT MOON.** This is the time to let go and declutter, or rest and reflect upon your accomplishments. Take in what you have done, and put away anything that didn't go well.

- At the end of each moon cycle (at **DARK MOON**) there is the opportunity to review, refresh and start again.

You can also journal the equinoxes and solstices that mark the four quarters of the year. In earlier times, when folk lived with more awareness of the progress of the seasons, these days were regarded as significant occasions for both reflection and celebration. By marking these days in your journal, you can align your journal work with the natural progression of the year. The autumn equinox is the most important, as it is nature's new year. There is the celebration of the final harvests coming in, and it is time to review what we achieved and what we want to improve on or continue. The winter solstice is the time of the lowest energy and the time when the days are short and the nights are long. This is the most introverted time, to withdraw, plan, dream, set up and create new journals and journal rituals and do the preparation work for what you want to achieve in the year ahead. At the spring solstice, we experience renewal and new growth, and begin to put our plans into action, and at the summer solstice, as the sun reaches its highest point, we are the most active and extroverted.

By working in sync with the moon cycles, you can make use of the way that the moon may be affecting you at different times, and enjoy the feeling that you are working in harmony with nature.

USE TAROT OR ORACLE CARDS AS JOURNAL PROMPTS

You can use a deck of tarot cards as a source of inspiration and direction in your journal work, and as a fun way to open up your insight and self-awareness. The tarot is a centuries-old system that still resonates with us because it is based on the timeless myth of the hero's journey through life, and all the experiences we have along the way. The tarot images represent instantly recognizable archetypes of human characters and situations. Tarot is more popular than ever in the 21st century, with fresh modern looks and interpretations, but the basic story and imagery are a system that has stood the test of time.

People across the world use tarot for their own purposes as a visual storyboard that can be applied to any situation. However, it is a story that has an ethical framework and ancient moral underpinnings, such as ideas about the meaning and purpose of the journey through life, karma and rebirth, hubris and that we reap what we sow in continuing and repeated cycles. There are countless tarot books and resources explaining the meanings of the cards, but you don't need to know about any of these interpretations to use tarot as a resource in your journal writing. What is important is the way in which you connect to or resonate with the archetypal image on a card in relation to your situation. Tarot is a handy tool that can help you make connections and build on your intuition by enabling you to step outside the box of your personal perceptions and see a bigger picture. It opens a doorway to the transpersonal or archetypal realm. You can use the images to activate the creative and intuitive side of your brain. You can build your own original links to apply the ideas held within the image to your situation as a form of creative problem-solving and self-reflection.

Each card holds both potential positive and negative interpretations, and if you draw a card upside down, the meaning is considered reversed. This means the message is more subdued, more internalized, or is in opposition to the upright meaning. Sometimes a reverse card can be a used as a warning to pay attention. If you want to include reversed readings — which is optional — then shuffle so that some cards are upside down.

Choose any tarot deck, but choose one with clear images. You can also use an oracle deck in the same way — it does not have to be a tarot deck, but make sure it is sufficiently detailed and has enough cards to give you a good choice. Choose a deck that you like; there is no point if you find the cards irritating or confusing!

SUGGESTIONS FOR USING TAROT CARDS AS JOURNAL PROMPTS

Shuffle and select three cards in the morning. The first card represents your foundation for the day, the second card represents how you will experience the day, and the third represents advice on how to deal with the day's themes.

Use tarot journalling to get unstuck when you need a new insight or perspective. When you feel at a loss about how to move forwards, draw a card and look at the situation from the perspective of the card. You can also draw a card to help answer a specific question, such as when you are seeking inspiration for your journalling or you are seeking a card to represent the foundation of an issue you are working with.

Set your focus for your journal writing time and then pick a card and ask how this card relates to your enquiry or concern. Allow the image on the card to spark new ideas, thoughts and connections about this topic.

If you are trying to gain clarity or make a decision, first write the question that is concerning you as clearly as you can. Then select a card and see what answers, insights and/or considerations might come, and write about them.

TAROT KEYWORDS FOR THE MAJOR ARCANA

The brief tarot card interpretations on the following pages are based upon the traditional Rider Waite Smith deck, the most widely used type of deck today. When drawing a card, decide in advance whether, in the situation you are thinking about, the cards are to represent you, the path or track you are currently on, whether they are to be used as advice to follow or to guard against, or whether the cards represent another person. To make this really clear, draw your cards in pre-decided spreads. Shuffle and deal your cards randomly, face down. If you are using a new deck you need to shuffle and cut the deck thoroughly so the cards are no longer in sequence. If you wish, you can separate out the 22 major arcana cards and just use these (for more detail on the arcana cards, see the following pages).

To give you a focus for today for today's writing or for a project: draw one major card to represent the current phase of your project and where you need to focus your energy and resources today.

When you are planning a project: select one card to represent the current phase of your project, one card to represent what you need to pay attention to along the way, and one card to represent how this project will look when you have completed it to the best of your ability. If needed, you can draw a fourth card to represent new ideas or advice to try.

To explore relationships, choose one card to represent yourself and place it in the middle. Choose one card to represent the other person, and one that represents your relationship.

Select one card each day and write, in the first person, about the main protagonist on the card, identifying with them as though they are you. Describe your life as this person, how you feel and think, what you are aware of, and what your concerns are.

MAJOR ARCANA MEANINGS

The 22 numbered cards of the major arcana depict the hero's journey from beginning to end, and the adventures, challenges, choices and dilemmas experienced along the way. The major arcana deal with the big archetypal themes in life, such as life lessons, big events, important changes and issues that require your attention.

The fool (0)

New beginnings, taking a risk and the need to assess the risk, starting out, hope, open-mindedness and also naivety. Birth is a special, sacred time as the hero takes on a form and steps into the unknown. The first seven major arcana cards depict the fool's journey through the material world; cards 8 to 14 show his world of emotions, connections and relationships; and cards 15 to 21 show his spiritual world, the consequences of his actions, and what he is learning about.

The magician (1)

Resources, raw materials and resourcefulness, power, skill, self-confidence and manifestation, making something happen. Creating success and a can-do attitude. Independence, inspiration and new ideas. Reversed, the magician suggests stagnation, poor planning or follow-through, or lack of attention to important details.

The high priestess (2)

Revealing the hidden. In order to continue on your journey, the high priestess suggests the need for quiet, solitary time for reflection and journal writing! She will offer you wisdom if you spend time listening in stillness to what is true and right for you, but if you do not spend the time, the wisdom will remain hidden. Her message is to trust your intuition. Reversed, this suggests a lack of reflectiveness, poor intuition or being unable to understand hidden information.

The empress (3)

A time to build, create and nurture. The empress is the ultimate image of the Great Mother — fruitfulness, creativity and maternal love. Look after your creations and your responsibilities with love and patience as they will mature and develop if you care for them. We all need this maternal aspect of life that takes us through our earthly cycles. It is an acknowledgment of your creative power and that you can attain what you desire. Reversed, it can indicate anxiety and concerns about dissatisfaction in life or relationships, fear of failure, lack of confidence, self-love and self-worth, worries and fears about infertility and infidelity, uncertainty in relationships, or lack of grounded connection to the earth.

The emperor (4)

The need for structure, stability, order and organization, the male principle. Security, the family, logic and squaring things up. Leadership is called for. Your goals and achievements need courage, foresight and planning with careful attention to all of the important structural details. Authority grounded in benevolent wisdom. Institutional power and authority. The importance of healthy routines. Reversed, the emperor can raise concerns about the misuse of authority, corruption, abuse of power, disorganization or overemphasis on personal needs at the expense of the needs of the group. It could also indicate lack of sufficient foresight, planning or attention to detail, or a male who is behaving in a way that is not mature or responsible.

The hierophant (5)

A trusted advisor, but one who can shake things up by making you question your foundations. This figure can look enigmatic to us today, but we need someone like this — someone who is able to offer sound advice based on tried and trusted thinking. This character shines a light that helps you find the truth of a situation, and also helps you discern the essential link between your beliefs and how you put them into practice in daily life. To find harmony, your beliefs about yourself and your actions need to be synchronized. Reversed, he can indicate a fear of change, misguided or rigid beliefs, judgment and discrimination.

The lovers (6)

This card suggests harmonious relationships of all kinds, including business partnerships. Love, harmony, beauty, decisions, listening to your heart, passion. It's about making choices, being able to trust your own choices, and being at one with your own higher self in the choices you make. Reversed, it can signify separation, lack of trust in oneself, or being overanalytical or rigid in your thinking.

The chariot (7)

By this stage in the journey, the fool has sought advice, made his choices and is riding ahead on his chariot, pushing ahead through obstacles. He is fired up by his own determination, focus and concentration, especially when different horses are pulling him in different directions, and he has to decide which way to go. Is your chosen route fulfilling your bigger purpose or is there an inner conflict tearing you apart? Reversed, this card signifies being stuck in a rut, lack of suitable preparation, or not setting off on the journey at all through resignation and giving up on your dreams.

Justice (8)

This is an opportunity to step back and take a long cool look at what is really needed right now — logically and objectively, rather than emotionally. The important principles of justice are balance, equality and fairness. Her gaze weighs up the choices you have made and the consequences of your actions. Are they balanced and appropriate or do you need to make some adjustments? Justice suggests a mindful and balanced centre, taking time for meditation. Reversed, the justice card suggests the storms of life may have thrown you a little off course and it may be time to recalibrate. It could also suggest you are suffering the effects of obstruction of justice, lack of equality and intolerance.

The hermit (9)

A time to pause, to withdraw into your own inner world for quiet observation, and the quest for inner peace and self-awareness. Time for reflective journalling. The light the hermit carries signifies the light of insight and inner wisdom. A hermit journalling exercise would be to make a list of the situations you want to resolve, so that you can go ahead and complete this phase. The hermit reversed suggests unfinished business, carelessness, situations lurking in the shadows that are calling for your attention before you can move on, lacking an inner compass or needing guidance.

The wheel of fortune (10)

This card signifies a new beginning, expansion, happiness and forward movement, taking the brakes off, a breakthrough. The wheel is a celebration of four virtues: knowledge, will, courage and inner silence. You are now ready for the unexpected discoveries, gifts and possibilities of your life to begin. Reversed, this can suggest being inflexible, not recognizing or making use of opportunities, or something standing in the way.

Strength (11)

You need your courage, inner strength, persistence and self-respect to win the day. This can refer to overcoming your own inner obstacles — such as challenging feelings — as much as external ones, or turning a perceived weakness into an advantage. Reversed, it suggests holding back, not living life to the full, wanting to get rid of inconvenient feelings, or not realizing your assets.

The hanged man (12)

A change in perspective, a delay, or time to hang out and wait, the need for patience and surrender, to face the truth, to see things clearly. A good opportunity for journalling, as you may be able to arrive at a fresh, new understanding.

Death (13)

An end and a beginning are interwoven and co-occurring, and you have reached a threshold of change. Letting something go means you can arise again, phoenix-like, from the ashes. How much choice do you have?

Temperance (14)

Listening within. Take time to discern what is really going on, and don't be impatient but wait to find a harmonious way forward.

The devil (15)

This dark and devilish image suggests bondage and compulsion, but the chains on the man and woman could easily be removed if they chose to do so. The situation might look bleak but you can simply walk away, and no one really has power over you unless you have allowed it.

The tower (16)

Change is necessary, and all that is non-essential will fall away to make way for the new. Sometimes this can be shocking, unexpected or radical change that is needed for renewal and regrowth.

The star (17)

After disruption, the star is a message of hope, offering timeless inspiration and pure values. Trust in yourself, and also take responsibility to live according to your true values or you can feel lost.

The moon (18)

It is easy to feel lost and confused, and the moon indicates a time of testing, or that you can't perceive things accurately due to your preconceptions about how things are. Try to get clear.

The sun (19)

Sunny and positive. Yes, you can feel gratitude, happiness and a sense that everything is working out. Don't forget to be optimistic and forward-moving.

Judgment (20)

In the clear light of day, the truth is revealed. The shrouded memories of the past are revealed as distortions. You are free to forgive and move on, as one day the truth will be plain for all to see. Hesitation and indecision do not serve you now.

The world (21)

A cycle completes and you have achieved a paradigm shift. Celebrate your success — or if you have not achieved success this time around, recollect the lessons of this cycle.

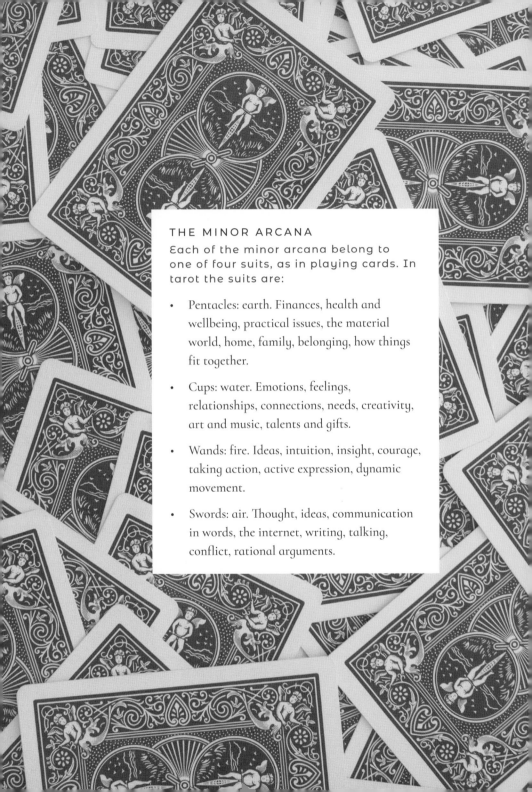

THE MINOR ARCANA

Each of the minor arcana belong to one of four suits, as in playing cards. In tarot the suits are:

- Pentacles: earth. Finances, health and wellbeing, practical issues, the material world, home, family, belonging, how things fit together.

- Cups: water. Emotions, feelings, relationships, connections, needs, creativity, art and music, talents and gifts.

- Wands: fire. Ideas, intuition, insight, courage, taking action, active expression, dynamic movement.

- Swords: air. Thought, ideas, communication in words, the internet, writing, talking, conflict, rational arguments.

The numbers of the suit cards correspond with traditional numerology:

- aces for new beginnings and the pure potential of being before matter comes into form
- twos for choices and partnerships, balance, duality and stasis
- threes for flux, a triangle, an outcome, a coming together, time to come together or get to work
- fours signify stability, a settled situation, possessions and belonging, a result
- fives bring instability, change, tension and conflict
- sixes suggest harmony, co-operation, and a continuation of the journey that is not yet complete
- sevens signify willpower, self-control and alignment
- eights suggest progress and strength
- nines signify fulfilment
- tens signify completion of a cycle.

If you combine the suit with the number you can apply the card to your situation, such as ten of cups. Ten is completion and cups is emotions, so this could describe a situation in which people come together in a happy way.

1876
BOLD
U.S.A. Order No
never forget yourself
GROW positive THOUGHTS
be
SMILE more
time is now
TAKE
a better me is COMING
STABILO BOSS
PAPER COPY FAX

PART 6

Final thoughts

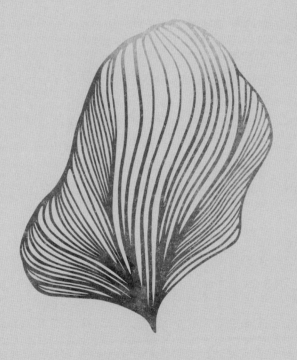

Your best ideas can come while you are journalling. Processing ideas with pen and paper is still the best way to solve problems and come up with new ideas, because when your mind is focused and intensely engaged you are much more likely to be creative.

CHAPTER 14

Troubleshooting and problem-solving

FORGETTING, GETTING STUCK, GIVING UP: WHEN JOURNAL WRITING IS NOT HAPPENING

- Why is it that you can have the intention to keep a journal regularly, but weeks go by in which you 'forget' to write anything?

- Do you buy blank books and then neglect them?

- Do you begin a journal with enthusiasm but then realize with dismay that you have 'nothing to say' or nothing interesting or important you want to write about?

- Do those blank pages that you are meant to fill, instead fill you with anxiety and panic?

- Does it feel self-indulgent/pointless to spend all this time writing about yourself?

- Are you impatient with yourself and easily bored, and it's hard for you to maintain consistency?

Things go wrong if your journal becomes irrelevant, and you stop being curious and excited about what will happen when you pick it up and begin to write. You forget all about it, you are inconsistent and don't follow through, or you don't feel good about your journal – maybe you vented a lot of sticky negative feelings and now you don't feel like going near it any more. Maybe you lost interest and moved on to other things. Maybe you had a time when you were so busy or preoccupied you felt you couldn't keep it up.

Your journal will not judge you if you don't show up for an appointment. You can always go back and start over. Sometimes it's better to start again with a fresh look in a new book.

WRITING WITHOUT RULES — CLAIM YOUR SELF-WORTH

If you feel uncomfortable about writing because you were made to feel bad about your writing at school, or you were pressured into following rules in writing that never worked for you, journalling is a way to reclaim your own writing voice. This book is not intended as another set of rules and requirements. No one will be judging what you write. Choose any suggestions that work for you, and write in any way you want. You don't have to use correct grammar or spelling, write in proper sentences or ask for permission to express your truth. If your inner critic is attacking you, take the opportunity to talk back, dialogue with them on the page, and tell them to back off and allow you the room you need to grow. Write from the heart to find your freedom.

PRIVACY IS ESSENTIAL

It is essential that your journal is private and never read by anyone without your permission. If you doubt its privacy even slightly, you will not feel secure and safe enough to be completely open and honest in your writing, explore absolutely any topic, and be free to reinvent yourself. You can discuss this with your family or people you live with and ask for their assurance that they will respect your privacy, and you can write on the front pages of your journal 'Please never read this without my permission'. If you do not feel secure, consider a locked box or drawer, or another secure or secret hiding place. Some specially designed journals can be microwaved and the writing will completely disappear if you write with the right pens (research this online so you don't start a fire by trying to microwave an ordinary paper book!). There are specially designed physical journals you can write in by hand, then upload the content to an app and erase the handwriting completely, so you can enjoy the benefits of handwriting without the physical storage issues. There are also apps where you can write with a stylus on a realistic paper background, and you can have a satisfying experience of writing by hand but no hard copy exists. You may prefer to use a password locked online journal, notebook or note-taking app. You will need to review your old physical journals from time to time and decide which ones to keep, so you are in control of what people read after you die.

There are other important considerations about keeping your work, your journals, your drafts, sketches and ideas private, even from those you love and who are dear to you and who you trust completely. A journal is your raw, unworked wrestling with yourself to nudge yourself ever onwards towards a more creative and productive mindset. Your journals are the physical location for the development of you and your material that happens in its own inexplicable, mysterious, unique way. Do you need or want to explain or justify any of this to anyone? Sometimes shoots that come up in the dark just need to be left alone until they are strong enough. You don't pull them up to examine their fragile little roots and comment that they don't look strong enough. It's unlikely to help if you discuss your ideas and the attitudes and mindsets you have worked so hard to create. When something is ready to come out into the world, it will be clear to you that you're ready, but before then don't seek approval or feedback. Don't explain about what you are doing in your journal, just say you are working something out and leave it at that.

This process of writing down information in communion with your inner self and letting it gestate before it comes into the world is recognized by writers and journallers the world over. The process of journalling steadily builds your self-belief and helps you work directly with your own creativity, but someone else's opinions about what you are doing can so easily stop you, as no one else can really understand what it is you are doing and what you get from it. It can even mean you can never get back to it in the same way. Your job when you are journalling is to create a special feeling and relationship with your work that builds and builds. Julia Cameron expresses this in *The Right to Write*, where she says there is a real risk if there is interruption in the private space of writing to and from your inner self: '… The self withdraws. The mind may remain, writing more and more cleverly and defensively, but the soul of the writing will vanish.'[1] She gives examples of friends who stopped being able to write because the opinions and views of others completely spoiled the process.

When you decide you are ready for feedback about your ideas or writing, ask someone who is able to value your work and see it for what it is, who can recognize what you are striving for and will support that. Ask them to give specific feedback to help you grow and develop, that will not make you feel defensive. The sensitivity and creativity that leads to innovative work is not always robust in the face of criticism. It is best only to ask for any feedback when you are done with the main creative phase, and you are a little detached from it. Think very carefully before inviting feedback from those closest to you.

REASONS FOR NOT JOURNALLING

I have heard many objections to journalling from clients and students over the years … mainly to do with lack of self-belief and thus a lack of trust in the journalling process. These are often an expression of impatience, resistance and fear towards the intensity, the focus, the consistency and the sheer power of journal writing process. You may feel some understandable reluctance about being drawn into a process that could be time consuming and involves facing yourself. Some people think that journalling is perhaps self-indulgent and a waste of time, or an activity reserved for teenaged girls. Surely important, busy people don't waste time on something so messy and personal?

I don't have the time, it would take too much time, I would rather just do my work and get on with my day than waste my time planning and thinking about it, I wouldn't remember to do it, I'm not able to do it every day, I don't like being consistent, I can't write, my handwriting is terrible, what's the point, I wouldn't know what to write, men don't journal, I wouldn't know where to start or how to make it useful, I started a journal a few times but it didn't really go anywhere.

It's true that not all types of journalling suit everyone, and this is why you need to find your own combination of methods. If you are a pragmatic, fact-oriented, results-focused type of person, your journals will be very different from those of an intuitive, reflective person who really enjoys life writing. However, journalling is a timeless resource that truly is available to everyone, no matter how you think, what you believe, how you vote, what groups you identify with, what language you write in, what you look like, or how you are judged or labelled in your society. For once, here is a level playing field that truly is for everyone who can read and write. Even if you have initial doubts, surrender to the journalling process and enjoy it, because journalling offers you a voice and a way to be more fully yourself.

I have heard clients and students express intense and possibly subconscious fears such as the fear of potential success, the fear of facing your fears, fear of paying attention to yourself, fear of directed and consistent work and effort, fear of commitment, fear of making mistakes or making a mess, fear of discovering more truth about yourself, impatience and lack of acceptance of yourself, massive self-doubt that anything worthwhile will emerge — or fear that someone else might read it. The only fear here that needs to be treated seriously is the fear of someone else reading what you have written. All the other fears can be worked through in the journalling process itself, and if you are motivated to grow and develop through them, you can do so. Each time you sit down to write, lightly nudge yourself towards a more positive mindset. Focus on whatever you can find that you have good feelings about — even if the only thing you can think of is one day in your life a long time ago — and write about that. You need to work patiently with deep fears and resistances, and not too directly, but never let them stand between you and the success you are capable of. Try one journalling approach and give yourself a chance by being consistent with it for a few weeks until you have sufficient experience to be able to evaluate the results. Remember you cannot judge the effectiveness of a journal by what your journalling work looks like, only by how it affects you in the longer term.

JOURNAL WRITER'S BLOCK

Everyone has felt intimidated by a blank white page or screen, a virgin notebook that seems too special to 'spoil' by writing in it, or when you just can't think of anything to say. I have heard experts claim that writer's block does not exist. In my experience it certainly does exist, but there is more than one cause, and more than one type of block. In order to fix or address what is stopping you from success with journalling or other writing, you first need to understand what is causing the difficulty.

FEAR OF THE BLANK PAGE

Journal writer's block can be described in various ways, such as the feeling that you don't know where to start, you have nothing to say, there is something you want to write but you don't know what it is, or you feel that what you want to write is not good enough. You feel inadequate, or you feel the whole thing is pointless, and you even feel a little despair about it. You feel stuck. You pick up your journal and then give up because you feel disheartened.

First of all, you need patience to stick with what you are feeling and not just give up. You also need to realize that whatever you are feeling is a key. It could, for example, be a form of anxiety. It may be quite normal to experience some anxiety whenever you sit down to write. So break down the anxiety into something specific and manageable. Telling yourself that it is difficult, or you can't do it, or criticizing or judging your output won't help. Instead, direct your attention to what you can write about — for just 5 minutes, describe something that you are aware of, then leave it at that for the day. Be flexible and spontaneous about the 'rules' of journal writing, but the advice given to writers by writers is generally to write a small amount every day, and to be patient with small but persistent output because this is a way of training yourself to accept where you are and value whatever comes. When you become experienced as a journal writer you realize that each sentence, paragraph and page you write is not an end in itself, but it clears the way for the next ideas and thoughts that are behind it, that cannot emerge until the space in front is cleared for them — like trains on a track emerging out of a tunnel. Perfectionism and expecting high standards of yourself is an enemy to productive journalling, especially when you are at the beginning stages of just needing to clear the track ahead of you so you can begin. Similarly, do not judge how your journal or your handwriting looks or if it is filled with stops, starts, mistakes, crossings out and coffee stains! As long as you keep showing up and you can read your own writing, this is all that matters.

When you hit dry times, remember everyone has days that are not productive. There are days for musicians when the violin squeaks, the voice is terrible. This is normal and it is not a reason to give up. There are cycles of productivity, alternating with times when you need to absorb and process, just as in winter the fields are left empty to rest before they are ploughed and reseeded in the early spring. These are days to seek inspiration and ideas. Craft a list of resources to explore when you need some input. However, beware of comparing yourself with other journallers, as this can be confusing and overwhelming. It's best to develop your own approach that works for you, and share methods and ideas once you feel more established. Days when you do not feel like writing are also good days for setting up new journals or for going through your old ones.

There is a reason for the structure of everyday practice, because this can hold you in place when things fall apart, you get busy or distracted, too much happens or you lose focus.

Once you have set a journal up, it will be there waiting for you on your return. No one is watching, no one is judging, and this is a personal, direct relationship with yourself. Try any of the journalling techniques in this book. Don't stop. Find something that works for you. Make some marks on the paper, write one small, insignificant thing. Write down the words of a song you just heard or what someone just said. Write a list. Start by writing about where you are in yourself, how you are feeling right now in the midst of all that is happening. Being blocked is often about not recognizing and not accepting how you feel, because the block itself is what you need to write about, can you but recognize it.

Journal writing is about changing something enormous: it is saying that how you feel and think matters and is important, that the small details of your own life are hugely significant, and that everything you feel and think is worthy of your time.

In a world where you may be told that you are not recognized or valued, claiming your unique value and self-respect is a lifeline to freedom and personal power. If you struggle to write because of how you feel, write about how you feel. There's a reason writing materials are so valued by people who are in prison, and why so much incredible writing has been produced by people who were — and are — incarcerated. Write to find that reason for yourself: how journalling makes you strong and free. Write to claim your confidence, self-worth and empowerment. Write to free your voice and your self-expression. If you can't find written words, use art journalling.

THE DISTILLED APPROACH OF THIS BOOK

If you have read or skimmed the book, you might be feeling a bit overwhelmed or confused and not sure where to start. Why not start with a simplified approach. When you place your trust in the journalling process, you can find any answers, solutions or results you seek. So start with journalling about your desires and thoughts about what you want from your journalling practice. Ask yourself questions about what you want to gain, learn and achieve from this process, and what you would like to change. Focus on something positive that you want to create, or a positive feeling you are seeking to expand and enjoy. Journalling is a way of taking small, imperfect daily action that over time builds momentum and power. Once you really get going, you will not want to stop.

Choose materials (or an app) that you will enjoy using and that look good. Create a pleasant ambience in the space where you will work. Commit to making this a healthy daily habit to enhance your sense of wellbeing. Make it fun, make journalling pleasant and enjoyable.

Your main focus needs to be to create a pleasant and uplifting ambience for your journalling sessions. Begin your sessions with a brief meditation or mindfulness practice session, where you listen to a background sound, or observe your breath — anything that helps you stop listening to your mental chatter and focus instead on feeling centred and grounded in your body. Relax, and allow a sense of spacious wellbeing to arise and expand. If you find yourself busy, stressed, anxious or unable to relax, then reduce the pressure by writing out the causes of this in a separate process, such as in a scribble or brain dump journal (see pages 74 and 75); or use the daily pages method (page 85) or some mindfulness journalling prompts (page 118).

Choose your first journalling topic and approach to give you results in the short to medium term, and begin with something you feel excited and optimistic about. From your initial exploration, drill down to just a few journalling topics to begin with until you are proficient at holding the focus of several different projects with sufficient depth of attention. It is the build-up of close, focused positive attention that makes journalling effective.

Write in your journal every day. Consistency builds momentum. Never give up. Never give in to negative voices because trust in the process itself creates the foundation for success. You are the original and unique author of your own life and projects and no one and nothing else can help line this up for you like your journalling practice.

JOURNAL FOR CHANGE: ESTABLISH YOUR INTENTIONS FOR YOUR JOURNALLING PRACTICE

Your journal is key in creating important changes and development in your work and life. In order to be even more successful than you are already, you need to follow a structured process whereby you can build coherence into every stage and aspect of your project. Journalling is a profoundly helpful activity because it entrains you to your success.

Success is not difficult
to achieve when you
bring in qualities
of determination,
consistency and
application.

This is where you can enlist your journal to do some of the
hard work for you as it becomes a thing in its own right. It's a
physical object, a location and a nexus for your thinking and
your work. It's full of you and your focus and intent — there is
nothing more powerful or effective to be found anywhere.

Bibliography

Carroll, Ryder, 2018, *The Bullet Journal Method: Track your past, order your present, plan your future*, New York, Fourth Estate.

Frank, Anne, 1947, 1997, *The Diary of a Young Girl: The definitive edition*, New York, Bantam (also available in many editions and languages worldwide).

Frankl, Victor, 2006, *Man's Search for Meaning*, Boston, Beacon Press, first published 1946.

Gardner, H., 1983, *Frames of Mind: The theory of multiple intelligences*, various editions and citations online.

Graf, Maria Christine, 2004, *Written emotional disclosure: A controlled study of the benefits of expressive writing homework in outpatient psychotherapy*, a thesis submitted to the faculty of Drexel University for Doctor of Philosophy Degree, available online.

Goldberg, Natalie, 1986, *Writing Down the Bones: Freeing the writer within*, Boston, Shambhala Publications.

Goleman, Daniel, 1997, *Emotional Intelligence: Why it can matter more than IQ*, New York, Bantam.

Hughes, Anne, 1981, *The Diary of a Farmer's Wife 1796–1797*, Anne Hughes, her boke in wiche I write what I doe, when I hav the tyme, and beginnen with this daye, Feb ye 6 1796, London, Penguin.

Kwik, Jim, *Kwik Student: Advanced study skills*, online training, Hay House and YouTube.

Lepore SJ: 'Expressive writing moderates the relation between intrusive thoughts and depressive symptoms.' *Journal of Personality and Social Psychology*. 1997, 73: 1030-1037 McCombie, Karen, 2004, *My V. Groovy Journal (Ally's World)*, London, Scholastic Press.

Pepys, Samuel, 1924 ed, *The Diary of Samuel Pepys*, 1669, London, Macmillan & Co.

Psychotherapy Research. 2008 Jul;18(4):389-99. doi: 10.1080/10503300701691664.

Ueland, Brenda, 1991, *If You Want to Write: Releasing your creative spirit*, Shaftesbury, Element Books.

Endnotes

CHAPTER 1

1. Phillip M. Ullrich and Susan K. Lutgendord, 2002, 'Journaling about stressful events: Effects of cognitive processing and emotional expression', *Annual of Behavioral Medicine*, University of Iowa.

2. Katherine M. Krpan, Ethan Kross, Marc G. Berman, Patricia J. Deldin, Mary K. Askren, and John Jonidesa, 2013, 'The benefits of expressive writing for people diagnosed with major depressive disorder', *Journal of Affective Disorders*, Sep 25; 150(3): 1148–51., published online, June 1810.1016/j.jad.2013.05.065.

3. Phillip M. Ullrich and Susan K Lutgendorf, 'Journaling about stressful events: Effects of cognitive processing and emotional expression', *Annals of Behavioral Medicine*, 24(3):244–50, February 2002.

4. K. Klein, and A. Boals, 2001, 'Expressive writing can increase working memory capacity', *Journal of Experiential Psychology Gen.*, Sep; 130(3): 520–33, Department of Psychology, North Carolina State University, Raleigh, USA.

CHAPTER 4

1. Clarke, Philip, 2017, University of Derby, quoted in https://www.telegraph.co.uk/health-fitness/body/common-new-years-resolutions-stick/

2. Bupa, 2015, https://www.bupa.co.uk/newsroom/ourviews/new-year-new-you

3. G.T. Doran, 1981, 'There's a S.M.A.R.T. way to write management's goals and objectives', Management Review, AMA Forum, Nov, 70 (11): 35–6.

CHAPTER 6

1. Julia Cameron, 2016, *The Artist's Way 25th Anniversary Edition*, New York, Penguin Random House LLC.

2. Kristy Conlin, *Art Journal Kickstarter: Pages and prompts to energize your art journals*, Ohio, North Light Publications.

CHAPTER 9

1. Alexis Blue, UANews, 'Narrative journaling may help heart's health post-divorce', https://uanews.arizona.edu/story/narrative-journaling-may-help-hearts-health-postdivorce. 8 May 2017.

2. Smith et al, The physical and psychological health benefits of positive emotional writing, Northumbria Research Link, http://nrl.northumbria.ac.uk.

3. Brandon Specktor, 'Writing a to-do list before bed could help you sleep', https://www.livescience.com/61422-journal-writing-sleep-better.html. 13 January 2018.

CHAPTER 10

1. Fernandes, M., Wammes, J., and Meade, M., 'The surprisingly powerful influence of drawing on memory', *Current Directions in Psychological Science*, 27(5), 302-308. https://doi.org/10.1177/0963721418755385. 30 August 2018.

CHAPTER 11

1. Ueland, Brenda, 1991, *If You Want to Write: Releasing your creative spirit*, Shaftesbury, Element Books.

CHAPTER 14

1. Julia Cameron, 1998, *The Right to Write: An invitation and initiation into the writing life*, London, Pan Macmillan.

Index